T0312130

COVID-19 and Entrepreneurship

Amid the COVID-19 pandemic, small businesses are especially vulnerable. This is one of the first books that explicitly examines the linkage between crisis and entrepreneurship with a specific focus on small businesses.

The book adopts a holistic approach and outlines strategies that small business owners can utilize as well as business opportunities that are available in these new market conditions. It also provides a comparative analysis of the current and future market conditions to enable a better understanding of how institutional structures can facilitate or hinder growth. The book also goes on to explain why and how creativity and innovation can help to mitigate the impact of such a crisis on business and highlights why business continuity is especially crucial to family-owned businesses.

This timely publication will help to guide small business owners and entrepreneurs to maintain business continuity and build up their resilience in a challenging business climate.

Vanessa Ratten is Associate Professor at La Trobe University, Australia.

COVID-19 and Entrepreneurship

Challenges and Opportunities
for Small Business

Edited by Vanessa Ratten

LONDON AND NEW YORK

First published 2021
by Routledge
2 Park Square, Milton Park, Abingdon, Oxon OX14 4RN

and by Routledge
52 Vanderbilt Avenue, New York, NY 10017

Routledge is an imprint of the Taylor & Francis Group, an informa business

British Library Cataloguing-in-Publication Data
A catalogue record for this book is available from the British Library

Library of Congress Cataloging-in-Publication Data
A catalog record for this book has been requested

ISBN: 978-0-367-71089-7 (hbk)
ISBN: 978-0-367-71087-3 (pbk)
ISBN: 978-1-003-14924-8 (ebk)

Typeset in Bembo
by Apex CoVantage, LLC

Contents

Figures

Tables

Contributors

Sandeep Bhasin is Associate Professor, Amity International Business School, Amity University Uttar Pradesh, India.

Ana Diogo is Professor at Higher Institute of Management and Administration of Leiria, Leiria, Portugal.

Clare D'Souza is Professor at La Trobe Business School, La Trobe University, Australia.

Aquilino Felizardo is Professor at Polytechnic Institute of Leiria, Leiria, Portugal and a Researcher member of CEFAGE-UÉ, Évora, Portugal.

Bhawna Kumar is Vice President at RBEF (Amity Education Group), India.

Vanessa Ratten is Associate Professor at La Trobe Business School, La Trobe University, Australia.

Eulália Santos is Professor at Polytechnic Institute of Leiria, Leiria, Portugal.

Andrea Sousa is Professor at Miguel Torga Higher Institute, Coimbra, Portugal and a researcher member of CEPESE, Porto, Portugal.

Fernando Tavares is Professor at Higher Institute of Business and Tourism Sciences, Porto, Portugal.

Ashleigh-Jane Thompson is Lecturer at La Trobe Business School, La Trobe University, Australia.

Esha Thukral is Lecturer at La Trobe Business School, La Trobe University, Australia.

Acknowledgments

This book has consumed much time and effort, which I have enjoyed, but also I am thankful to a number of people who made this possible. First, I thank Yongling Lam, who provided very helpful suggestions and feedback about the book. Her knowledge and expertise are very much appreciated. As this book has been written during the COVID-19 pandemic, there have been many ups and downs during this time. Initially, I thought the COVID-19 pandemic would last a short time; however, this has proved to be incorrect as the pandemic has continued. Living in Melbourne, Australia, we have faced some of the harshest lockdown restrictions in the world, which have limited activities but at the same time, this has been good for writing. Therefore, I thank my family for being with me during this time especially my dad David Ratten, brothers Stuart Ratten and Hamish Ratten, sister-in-law Tomomi Ratten, and my niece Sakura Ratten.

During this time of the COVID-19 pandemic, we are still uncertain as to how, if, and when the world will change. It is similar in scenario to many of the books; my mum Kaye Ratten used to love to read, who unfortunately is not here anymore but still around in a spiritual way. I remember her discussing with my brothers about the Global Financial Crisis in 2009, which was a major crisis that affected the world but did not have the same health connotations as the current COVID-19 crisis.

Most of this book has been compiled, written, and edited during the 2020 Melbourne lockdown, which lasted for a long time and is viewed by some as being one of the longest lockdowns in the world. The Melbourne lockdown lasted most of the Australian winter and severely affected economic and social life. Never before had the same level of geographic restrictions been in place for individuals in Australia. Many state borders were closed and as many of the COVID-19 Australian cases have been in Melbourne, it significantly affected the city. As I live and work in Melbourne, it was amazing to see the solidarity in the community.

Hopefully, the chapters in this book will provide inspiration, help, and guidance to small businesses dealing with the current environmental changes caused by COVID-19. Entrepreneurship provides a positive way to manage change and it is hoped that small businesses will look to the more positive associations of change resulting from the pandemic. This includes an increased emphasis on digital capabilities and innovation in order to survive in the global marketplace.

1 COVID-19, entrepreneurship, and small business

Vanessa Ratten

Introduction

Since the start of the COVID-19 pandemic in January 2020, small businesses have had to significantly change in order to survive (Heyden, Wilden and Wise, 2020). Many small businesses have had to terminate full-time employees or change working relationships due to COVID-19. This has resulted in a significant number of individuals working from home or reducing their normal work hours. COVID-19 is a new crisis that has affected small business like nothing else in recent history (Cortez and Johnson, 2020). In general terms, the COVID-19 crisis is about the challenges and opportunities small businesses in particularly face from changed environmental conditions. The challenges arise from the need for social distancing and online capabilities along with the emotional changes in human behavior, while the opportunities refer to new market needs (Donthu and Gustafsson, 2020). To support better and more timely decision-making in the COVID-19 crisis, small businesses need to rethink their current market strategies to create solutions for COVID-19-related problems (Kraus, Clauss, Breier, Gast, Zardini and Tiberius, 2020).

As the role of small business is integral to the success of the global economy, it is important to understand how the COVID-19 crisis has changed society. Due to the COVID-19 crisis, there is an opportunity and a need for small businesses to redefine who they are and what markets they serve. This opportunity needs to be addressed as small businesses face significant challenges. What is the way forward for small business? Small businesses need to confront the issues raised by the COVID-19 crisis. This may involve redefining the purpose of small business in light of the crisis in terms of how they sell and source products or services. Small businesses have special qualities that can be vital to the survival of a community, but they need to be prepared for change. Those who work for and in a small business are confronting numerous challenges, but by having a positive attitude, they can survive and prosper from the crisis. This means they need to be aware of the conflicts and dilemmas faced by small business by utilizing an entrepreneurial mindset.

Small businesses are a central part of entrepreneurship studies and there is a large body of literature existing on this topic. The research on COVID-19 and small business is new and only now emerging due to the significance of the pandemic on society (Kuckertz, Brändle, Gaudig, Hinderer, Reyes, Prochotta and Berger, 2020). Small businesses are a significant economic force and play a key social role in society. This means that COVID-19 and small business are a subject worthy of consideration and inquiry due to how it has changed business practices.

Although the impact of the COVID-19 pandemic on entrepreneurship is obvious, it seems necessary to explain it in more detail. This will allow further elaboration on what factors persuade small businesses to adopt a cooperative approach to entrepreneurship. The questions then worth asking and that are answered in this book are: how do small businesses utilize cooperative entrepreneurship during the COVID-19 pandemic and how is it distinguished from other types of entrepreneurship? In this chapter, it seeks to bring together extant work on COVID-19 and entrepreneurship by advancing the research on this topic. This chapter highlights the changes in entrepreneurship practice caused by COVID-19 and how entrepreneurial activities will change. The chapter also discusses how small business entrepreneurship will change in the future by providing an overview of the challenges faced by small businesses in the COVID-19 pandemic. This will enable a better understanding of the role of small business in the global economy and the impact of entrepreneurship in times of crisis. It also provides a discussion on the small business sector and its ability to respond to environmental change.

Nature of small business

Small businesses have advantages over large businesses due to the more interactive nature of relationships within the business structure (Santos, Marques and Ratten, 2019). This enables faster and more direct contact between owners, employees, and customers. At the same time, there are also disadvantages associated with small businesses due to their resource-constrained environment (Scase, 2012). Small businesses are able to serve niche markets not served by large businesses. This enables a closer connection to communities in terms of the types and kinds of products or services offered. Large businesses often operate on mass production models and are unable to specialize. This means that unlike large businesses, small businesses can offer smaller sized quantities of products and more individualized service (Anggadwita, Ramadani, Luturlean and Ratten, 2016). This enables products to be quickly adapted on the basis of consumer needs.

Small businesses comprise the majority of all enterprises in society and contribute significantly to the economic growth rate. There is no universally accepted definition of small business as it normally depends on the context. Definitions can vary based on the way small businesses are understood in the economy. Generally small businesses can be defined on the basis of the number of employees and turnover. This means businesses are considered small when compared to larger businesses they have less employees and assets. Although some view a small business as being an enterprise that is independently owned and managed.

Businesses are classified as being small when they have a lower level of employees and revenue than other businesses. Small businesses vary in terms of regulation depending on their geographic position. Small businesses that have a physical store or office location are governed by local regulations. Increasingly, small businesses that are digital based can operate from any location and are more difficult to regulate. In addition, during the COVID-19 pandemic, more small business owners and employees are working from home. Some small businesses do not have a growth motive and are happy with their current market position. The advantage of small businesses is that they can be started at a low cost and develop based on market need. This means initially the development of a small business will be a response to market conditions that determine if it increased in size or stays the same. Individuals are motivated to start a small business because it brings them financial revenue while pursuing market opportunities.

Small businesses are characterized by their normally independent nature in the marketplace. This means they are mostly operated by owners and do not have a dominant market position. Small business owners normally rely on their business as their main source of income. This means the business consumes the majority of the owner's time and energy. It is necessary to define a small business in order to clear about how it is affected by the COVID-19 pandemic and entrepreneurship. A small business is classified as a business with ownership held by an individual or a small group of individuals. This means their operations are mostly local and they contribute to the development of a community.

The majority of small business owners work on a full-time basis in the business. Most discussion on COVID-19 has focused on business in general without considering the intricacies of the small business sector (Alon, Farrell and Li, 2020). This means the existing literature on COVID-19 and entrepreneurship takes a predominately general perspective. More attention is needed on how small business owners have responded to the COVID-19 pandemic and the entrepreneurial decisions they have made. Measuring the resilience of small businesses during the COVID-19 pandemic is important (Bacq, Geoghegan, Josefy, Stevenson and Williams, 2020). The ways small businesses have been entrepreneurial will be based on the personal circumstances of the owners and their ability to adapt. With this in mind, this book will seek to explore the following questions related to COVID-19, entrepreneurship, and small business.

Small businesses often are started for low cost and on a part-time basis. Sometimes the reason for starting a small business involves pursuing a hobby or interest that can also produce an economic income. These small businesses are referred to as lifestyle businesses due to the way they combine lifestyle pursuits into financial outcomes. The internet has changed the way small businesses compete in the global marketplace as it has made it easier for them to advertise and sell their services. Prior to the internet being introduced into society, it was difficult for small businesses to establish themselves in international marketplaces. The internet changed this by making it cheaper and more time effective for small businesses to operate in an international marketplace. In addition, electronic and mobile commerce further transformed the shift in small businesses to an online environment.

Small businesses play an important role in the social fabric of society. They do this by providing services that are sometimes neglected by large businesses. Small businesses tend to have an independent nature and do not have to report to others. This is not always the case though with many small businesses operating under a franchise model or belonging to a national federation or association of small business owners. Having independence enables a small business to make their own decisions without interference. This enables them to quickly change market direction and to reap the rewards of their efforts (Ansell and Boin, 2019). However, it also brings challenges as small businesses take their own risks and do not have the financial support of large companies if they make a wrong decision.

Small firms tend to infrequently utilize research and development processes for product innovation. This is due to their small nature and inability to pay for such processes. However, small firms can test concepts quickly to assess the viability of products. This means they can utilize market testing methodologies in order to refine ideas. This leads to better innovations that are then assessed through market analysis. Small businesses have a try-and-see approach when understanding whether an idea will work in the market. Due to small businesses having a limited geographic market, they tend to have more local consumers. This means they are connected to a community in a way large businesses are not able to do. Small businesses can utilize their community linkages to build better business initiatives.

Small businesses have a financial fragility that means they do not have enough money to survive during the lockdown periods (Cankurtaran and Beverland, 2020). As the monthly expenses of small businesses assume a repeat and constant supply of customers, the lockdown substantially changes this assumption. Thus, it is impossible for small businesses to come out of the COVID-19 crisis unchanged (Chesbrough, 2020). The enormous change in terms of economic and psychological stress is likely to be felt for a long time period. This means that the pace at which the COVID-19 pandemic occurred has been distressing for all businesses, but especially more for small business. The toll of the crisis on small business is hard to estimate due to the ferocity of the COVID-19 crisis and its quick spreading nature representing an unprecedented event.

Entrepreneurship and small business

The word 'entrepreneur' can be analyzed in terms of its historical origins. Sarri and Trihopoulou (2005:26) states that 'the Latin roots of the word are entre meaning "enter," per meaning "before" and neur meaning "nerve center".' This means that an entrepreneur is classified as someone who disrupts current market conditions. This disruption occurs in the form of business activities that are new in nature. Entrepreneurship can be referred to as 'a person's commitment to capital accumulation and to business growth' (Scase, 2012:14).

This definition means that there is a deliberate goal to build wealth which differs from a proprietorship that refers more to ownership. The concept of entrepreneurship is ambiguous and has been considered from various perspectives. The phenomenon of entrepreneurship refers to beneficial change that has an economic impact (Doern, Williams and Vorley, 2019). Thus, entrepreneurship can be understood in a wide and narrow sense. In the wide sense, entrepreneurship refers to anything that is innovative and risk-taking. This means it is a general understanding of behavior that is considered futuristic and not normal. In the more narrow sense, entrepreneurship refers to a mindset that can be characterized by specific forms of behavior. This means the way entrepreneurship is measured and defined is different to ordinary types of activity. Entrepreneurship plays an important function in society by enabling new business ideas to take shape.

An entrepreneur differs to a proprietor by investing in pursuing opportunities that do not have a certain outcome. Proprietorship is defined as 'the ownership of property and other assets such that, although these can but not necessarily, be used for trading purposes and therefore to realise profits, are not utilised for the purpose of longer term processes of capital accumulation' (Scase, 2012:14). Entrepreneurs hope that the opportunities they pursue are manifested into productive outcomes, but sometimes their efforts are not necessarily rewarded. This means that there is a degree of risk inherent within any form of entrepreneurial activity. The difference between proprietors and entrepreneurs is that proprietors consume surpluses instead of reinvesting them like entrepreneurs do (Sarri and Trihopoulou, 2005). Increasingly there is an emphasis by small business proprietors to act entrepreneurially in order to insert in future trends. This enables their business to survive and to take advantage of technological change.

Entrepreneurship is a unique field of research, but the concept remains difficult to study. This is due to entrepreneurship being an elusive topic and philosophical debates existing about its definition. The nature of entrepreneurship in small business has dominated the scholarly conversation. In order to understand the role entrepreneurship plays in small businesses, it is useful to analyze the impact of organizational culture. The way things are done in a small business can be referred to as its culture. More specifically, an organizational culture can be defined as 'the deeply seated (often subconscious) values and beliefs shared by personnel in an organisation' (Martins and Terblanche, 2003:65). Entrepreneurship is part of an organization's culture and is manifested in behavior. This means an organization with a high level of entrepreneurship in its culture will likely engage in more risk-taking activities. The attitudes of individuals in the organization will be more risk-taking and want to engage in futuristic thinking. An organization's culture is integral to the effective functioning of an organization and ensures everyone is on the same track. By having shared values, it enables individuals to coordinate different activities. This helps to promote a sense of identity for individuals working in the organization.

Organizations use different processes to guide entrepreneurial behavior (Marques, Santos, Ratten and Barros, 2019). This means managerial tools that encourage entrepreneurial change play a key role in influencing behavior. Organizations can express an entrepreneurial attitude through their physical settings and artifacts (Jones, Jones, Williams-Burnett and Ratten, 2017). This includes the use of open plan offices that facilitate the exchange of ideas. Moreover, the meaning behind language utilized in an organization can have an entrepreneurial feel. This enables the communication and interpersonal relationships to emphasize innovation.

The expressive practice of culture is embedded in processes including the goals and strategic direction of an organization. This enables an organization to structure its mission around what is formally announced and what actually takes place. Stimulating entrepreneurship among small businesses is a noticeable feature of the small business policy agenda regarding the COVID-19 crisis. In the wake of the COVID-19 disturbances, promulgating entrepreneurship is an important means of maintaining social harmony. For the most part, small businesses remain the best way of tackling economic change and promoting entrepreneurship as a way to recover from the COVID-19 crisis (Sheth, 2020). Small businesses with entrepreneurial skills are able to act upon new business opportunities by exploiting market needs. Economic growth and societal well-being are influenced by the ability of small businesses to be entrepreneurial. Small business practitioners can ensure that entrepreneurial skills are used to spur performance.

COVID-19 and entrepreneurship

COVID-19 is a highly transmissible disease that has rapidly spread around the world (World Health Organization, 2020). The amount of research on COVID-19 entrepreneurship will increase exponentially in the next few years. The field will be further legitimized by the increase in interest in the topic and the publication of specialized books and special journal issues. Moreover, there will be heightened interest on COVID-19 entrepreneurship from the recognition that it is a distinct subject area. This is because COVID-19 entrepreneurs must cope with the unique interaction between crisis and context. This means COVID-19 entrepreneurship research is an appealing context for studying new forms of entrepreneurship. Considering that most businesses have been affected by COVID-19, omitting this topic from entrepreneurship discussions will lead to an incomplete knowledge base. Surprisingly there is little work done on the effects of crises on entrepreneurship. Thus, studying the COVID-19 crisis can contribute to important new insights into the issues mainstream entrepreneurship scholars are grappling with.

Small businesses are managed with the intention to pursue the mission of the business. There has been a sudden drop in the general supply and demand of most products. The widespread lockdown of many regions around the world led to a rise in demand for some products, but a decrease for others. The complex impact of the COVID-19 crisis on small business is difficult to assess but it has necessitated innovations that have enabled small businesses to survive the crisis (Hall, Scott and Gössling, 2020). The pandemic represents an opportunity for small business to digitize their operations. To do this, a small business needs to recognize the potential of digital business. This means focusing on working with new partners in the digital environment.

The COVID-19 disease continues to spread around the world with many countries experiencing a second wave of infections (He and Harris, 2020). Due to the health impacts of the virus, many governments have focused on saving lives instead of economic effects. This has placed an emphasis on health outcomes rather than the effects of the crisis on small business. The COVID-19 crisis has impacted the health, well-being, and economic sustainability of society (Jamal and Budke, 2020). Therefore, it is important to explore how small businesses have been affected as they represent a large proportion of total business. Small businesses are a core component of any economy. Most businesses start as small businesses that then grow or stay the same depending on market demand. Therefore, it is interesting to think about how the world will look after COVID-19 if that eventuates particularly in terms of the nature of small businesses (Kirk and Rifkin, 2020). At the moment, we are still in the midst of the COVID-19 pandemic with no vaccine or cure available. Thus, assuming a post-COVID-19 world means there is an assumption that there will be a medical way to deal with the virus. If this does not eventuate, the world will continue to live in a COVID-19 environment.

The success and survival of small businesses during the COVID-19 crisis depend on creativity and inventiveness. An effective reaction to the changed circumstances from COVID-19 leads to innovative changes that ensure the existence of small businesses. It appears that the rate of change is accelerating as new business methods are needed to deal with COVID-19 changes. Idea generation and new knowledge have a role to play in this change process. Small business leaders need to try and create a framework in which entrepreneurship is accepted as a basic cultural norm. This will emphasize the importance of entrepreneurship and stimulate new ideas.

COVID-19 entrepreneurship is defined as entrepreneurship that is designed in a way that suits the new environmental conditions. COVID-19 entrepreneurship can be also referred to as 'crisis entrepreneurship,' 'entrepreneurship during times of uncertainty,' and 'opportunity entrepreneurship.' Central to all of these terms is the need to reconsider how entrepreneurship occurs in the marketplace. COVID-19's effect on entrepreneurship will be extensive. COVID-19 entrepreneurship is an influential concept for business policy. There is a growing recognition that COVID-19 presents a fundamental transformation to society. Entrepreneurship is often viewed as a panacea for crises affecting the global economy. There remains considerable uncertainty regarding how entrepreneurs will deal with the COVID-19 crisis. To date the research on COVID-19 entrepreneurship has been sparse. There is a gap in our knowledge about how entrepreneurs will cope with the COVID-19 crisis. Awareness is growing that entrepreneurs are needed if the global economy is going to cope with the COVID-19 crisis.

The entrepreneurship process has tended to be a 'black box' as it is poorly understood. This is due to the complex nature of entrepreneurship in society. The way entrepreneurship develops and is implemented over time depends on the context. This knowledge gap is especially acute at the moment during the COVID-19 crisis when entrepreneurship is being utilized in different ways. There are a number of inputs that go into the process of entrepreneurship including knowledge and investment. The type and level of these inputs will differ depending on the urgency of the situation. Some inputs such as finance might be more important than others depending on the nature of the entrepreneurial business. This means it is useful to focus on the type of business venture in terms of its size to understand the entrepreneurship process. The outputs of entrepreneurship are normally evaluated in terms of performance. This means an increase in profitability or market share is the main output desired from businesses involved in entrepreneurship. Learning is also an outcome from entrepreneurship and can in the long term lead to other benefits. Increasingly the entrepreneurship process is dynamic and characterized by a multitude of relationships. This dynamic nature means that entrepreneurship can occur via relationships that are an integral part of the market environment.

Entrepreneurship is a dual process as it involves innovation and creativity. During the entrepreneurial journey, entrepreneurs transform ideas into commercialized products or services. The time that this process takes depends on the sequence of events and customer feedback. Some product ideas are easier to enter the market because of a lack of a viable alternative. This means transforming the product idea into an implemented reality is made easier. The entrepreneurship process tends to involve the following steps: idea generation, information dissemination, and relationship building (Ratten and Jones, 2020). In generating an idea, timing can play a role in its success. Some ideas are well timed and can fit into existing market structures, while others may require customers to adjust. This means when generating an idea, consideration is needed about how the idea will progress (Ratten and Braga, 2019). To do this, information needs to be disseminated among market participants as a way of gaining feedback and help. This process will serve as a way to improve the likelihood of the idea being successful in the market. Relationships are part of this process and are increasingly needed in the interlinked commercial environment especially in times of crisis (Williams, Gruber, Sutcliffe, Shepherd and Zhao, 2017).

Entrepreneurship starts with an idea that has the potential to develop into a business venture. Entrepreneurs assess each idea based on its market appeal. Part of this process involves creativity in terms of focusing on potential opportunities in times of crisis (Weick and Sutcliffe, 2011). The creative process involves "'kaleidoscope thinking" to rearrange existing "pieces" to create a new possibility' (Rodriguez-Sanchez, Williams and Brotons, 2019:879). This reference to a kaleidoscope means that there is a need to see things differently in terms of market potential. By focusing on possibilities instead of current market conditions, there is a sense of futuristic thinking. This enables entrepreneurs to recognize opportunities then to pursue them in the marketplace. Opportunity recognition involves two main phases: discovery and evaluation (Rodriguez-Sanchez et al., 2019). The discovery process then involves detecting and assessing new market trends. This process involves analyzing socioeconomic data in order to think about new market needs. To do this can be difficult as it involves thinking outside the box.

As there has been little empirical work to date on COVID-19 and entrepreneurship, there are many potential research avenues. Entrepreneurship scholars need to shift away from a focus on specific types of entrepreneurship to a more detailed general understanding about how COVID-19 has changed entrepreneurship. Later when the research on COVID-19 entrepreneurship is more established can researchers then conduct more specialized types of study. Arguably the study of COVID-19 entrepreneurship is poised to make an important contribution to the entrepreneurship scholarship and practice. This will enable new insights to emerge about the process of entrepreneurship but also enable a better understanding of underappreciated areas of entrepreneurship in times of crisis (Wenzel, Stanske and Lieberman, 2020). To do this, COVID-19 entrepreneurship research requires methodological and theoretical innovation. Scholars should be ready for this challenge as COVID-19 entrepreneurship provides a new frontier. The shift toward COVID-19 entrepreneurship research will require an understanding of the economic, social, and technological change that has hindered or supported entrepreneurship. In order to legitimize COVID-19 research, there needs to be an increase in the volume and rigor of studies (Parnell, Widdop, Bond and Wilson, 2020). There is not yet an accepted and consistent definition of COVID-19 entrepreneurship. Much of the existing research has been done in a quick time period and is exploratory in nature. This means it is difficult to articulate patterns in the research on COVID-19 and to formulate theories. Anecdotal evidence suggests that COVID-19 entrepreneurship is a unique form of entrepreneurship.

Implications

Small business managers can lead by example by promoting a culture of entrepreneurship. Due to the criticality of small businesses impact from the COVID-19 pandemic, it is necessary for more small business owners to act in an innovative manner. This means that small businesses need to clearly establish an orientation toward entrepreneurship in order to produce more fruitful outcomes. It is imperative that small business communities communicate an entrepreneurial spirit in response to the COVID-19 crisis. This can be done in the form of an entrepreneurial mission statement integrated into a small business strategy. In doing so, more entrepreneurial projects can be undertaken by small businesses. If small business owners are to elevate their entrepreneurship, they must redefine their strategy. Rather than continuing with their existing strategy, they need to accept the premise that the world has changed because of the COVID-19 crisis. Entrepreneurship in small business must adhere to a set of guidelines that promote innovation. This will simplify not only decision-making but also stress entrepreneurship.

Small business managers should create a comprehensive entrepreneurial stance that enables new thinking to take place. This means when faced by a specific decision, an established policy can provide the most appropriate response. A definitive policy on entrepreneurship will enable entrepreneurship to be viewed as a good strategy. Small business managers in both an individual and collective sense have an opportunity to be more entrepreneurial. This will increase the use of entrepreneurial behavior in a range of industries. Different industries must define entrepreneurship in terms of culture. This will help build more entrepreneurial practices in industry settings. Given the overall impact of COVID-19, it appears a suitable time for small businesses to respond in an entrepreneurial manner. There needs to be an entrepreneurial response to communicate more frequently and specifically on COVID-19-related issues. If small businesses do not promote entrepreneurship, it seems likely that there will be a further erosion of business goals. This means that small businesses have a responsibility for developing an entrepreneurial position in the marketplace.

Small businesses because of their independence need to often work long hours in order to survive. This can have positive outcomes in terms of having freedom to make their own decisions but can also affect work/life balance. There is a gap in the literature in terms of a comprehensive and recent investigation of small businesses and their attitudes toward entrepreneurship in the current COVID-19 market environment. This chapter seeks to correct this gap by addressing the following research questions:

1) To what extent do small businesses utilize entrepreneurship because of the COVID-19 crisis?
2) What specific entrepreneurial strategies have caused the best outcome for small businesses during the COVID-19 crisis?
3) How does entrepreneurship in small business differ in times of crisis and noncrisis?
4) What stakeholder groups do small businesses believe most influence the entrepreneurial response to the COVID-19 crisis?
5) How do small businesses react to the COVID-19 crisis in terms of entrepreneurship?

Conclusions

A number of conclusions can be drawn from this chapter in terms of the ability of small businesses to cope with the COVID-19 crisis. More small business entrepreneurs tend to believe that dramatic shifts in current operating models are needed to deal with the uncertainty caused by the COVID-19 crisis. Conflicts between past practices and current changes are to be expected. This means small businesses must change in accordance with COVID-19 regulations. In regard to issues such as human resource decisions, there are also likely to be some changes. This means small businesses need to consider ethical issues regarding COVID-19 required change.

This chapter offers the first truly comprehensive assessment of COVID-19 entrepreneurship research. The development of COVID-19 entrepreneurship practice and research will focus on two main pathways. One will examine the difference in entrepreneurship pre-, during, and post-COVID-19. This means research will focus on how the environmental context has changed as a result of the crisis. The other centers on developing a new theory of COVID-19 entrepreneurship based on new market conditions. The current state of the research offers ample opportunity for research in both streams. This chapter has provided an analysis of potential future practice and research directions regarding COVID-19 entrepreneurship. However, it is important to note that the relative newness of COVID-19 entrepreneurship as a concept is one of its limitations. This means research and practice are still in the evolution stage and therefore researchers need to be careful with generalizations.

The use of entrepreneurship policy to alleviate problems caused by COVID-19 by governments has been recognized in the media. Unfortunately from an academic point of view, research in the field of COVID-19 entrepreneurship is limited. This is due to there being a wide diversity of approaches to study COVID-19 and they can be distinguished in terms of an innovation or entrepreneurship focus. The innovation perspective stresses the need for change because of the COVID-19 pandemic. This means innovation can be considered from an incremental or radical point of view. Incremental innovation means that small changes can be made to suit the new market environment. These changes can be further refined on the basis of feedback from market participants. Thereby enabling improved products and services to be made. Radical innovation suggests more major changes that can take time to implement. The entrepreneurship perspective suggests that new business ventures are required because of the COVID-19 crisis. This means the economy needs profit-generating activities to finance value-creation activities.

Despite the importance of the COVID-19 crisis on small business, there is relatively little serious academic research into the topic. This chapter has set out to stimulate the discussion around this topic to fill the knowledge gap. The origins and evolution of entrepreneurship based on the COVID-19 crisis were discussed. In addition, the need to redefine a small business is something that has been done before, most notably during the first, second, third, and fourth industrial revolutions but needs to be done again because of the COVID-19 crisis. As one of the first comprehensive reviews on COVID-19 and entrepreneurship, this chapter has collated research examining the impact of a health crisis on society. This included examining the emergence of the COVID-19 crisis and how strategies regarding entrepreneurship have evolved. By covering the impact of COVID-19 on entrepreneurship, this chapter has discussed insights about what the changes mean for small business. It can be concluded that COVID-19 entrepreneurship research is gaining popularity among scholars, practitioners, and policy makers. This is due to COVID-19 entrepreneurship being quite different from traditional entrepreneurship theory. This means there is a lot of scope to create new theories and practices related to COVID-19 entrepreneurship.

References

Alon, I., Farrell, M. and Li, S. (2020) 'Regime type and Covid-19 response', *FIIB Business Review*, 1–9.

Anggadwita, G., Ramadani, V., Luturlean, B. and Ratten, V. (2016) 'Socio-cultural environments and emerging economy entrepreneurship: Women entrepreneurs in Indonesia', *Journal of Entrepreneurship in Emerging Economies*, 9(1): 85–96.

Ansell, C. and Boin, A. (2019) 'Taming deep uncertainty: The potential of pragmatist principles for understanding and improving strategic crisis management', *Administration & Society*, 51(7): 1079–1112.

Bacq, S., Geoghegan, W., Josefy, M., Stevenson, R. and Williams, T. (2020) 'The Covid-19 virtual idea blitz: Marshalling social entrepreneurship to rapidly respond to urgent grand challenges', *Business Horizons*, In Press.

Cankurtaran, P. and Beverland, M. (2020) 'Using design thinking to respond to crises: B2B lessons from the 2020 Covid-19 pandemic', *Industrial Marketing Management*, 88: 255–260.

Chesbrough, H. (2020) 'To recover faster from Covid-19, open up: Managerial implications from an open innovation perspective', *Industrial Marketing Management*, In Press.

Cortez, R. and Johnson, W. (2020) 'The coronavirus crisis in B2B settings: Crisis uniqueness and managerial implications based on social exchange theory', *Industrial Marketing Management*, In Press.

Doern, R., Williams, N. and Vorley, T. (2019) 'Special issue on entrepreneurship and crises: Business as usual? An introduction and review of the literature', *Entrepreneurship & Regional Development*, 31(5–6): 400–412.

Donthu, N. and Gustafsson, A. (2020) 'Effects of Covid-19 on business and research', *Journal of Business Research*, In Press.

Hall, C. M., Scott, D. and Gössling, S. (2020) 'Pandemics, transformations and tourism: Be careful what you wish for', *Tourism Geographies*, In Press.

He, H. and Harris, L. (2020) 'The impact of Covid-19 pandemic on corporate social responsibility and marketing philosophy', *Journal of Business Research*, 116: 176–182.

Heyden, M., Wilden, R. and Wise, C. (2020) 'Navigating crisis from the backseat? How top managers can support radical change initiatives by middle managers', *Industrial Marketing Management*, 88: 305–313.

Jamal, T. and Budke, C. (2020) 'Tourism in a world with pandemics: Local-global responsibility and action', *Journal of Tourism Futures*, In Press.

Jones, P., Jones, A., Williams-Burnett, N. and Ratten, V. (2017) 'Let's get Physical: Stories of entrepreneurial activity from Sports coaches/instructors', *International Journal of Entrepreneurship and Innovation*, 18(4): 219–230.

Kirk, C. P. and Rifkin, L. S. (2020) 'I'll trade you diamonds for toilet paper: Consumer reacting, coping and adapting behaviors in the Covid-19 pandemic', *Journal of Business Research*, In Press.

Kraus, S., Clauss, T., Breier, M., Gast, J., Zardini, A. and Tiberius, V. (2020) 'The economics of Covid-19: Initial empirical evidence on how family firms in five European countries cope with the corona crisis', *International Journal of Entrepreneurial Behavior & Research*, In Press.

Kuckertz, A., Brändle, L., Gaudig, A., Hinderer, S., Reyes, C. A. M., Prochotta, A. and Berger, E. S. (2020) 'Startups in times of crisis – A rapid response to the Covid-19 pandemic', *Journal of Business Venturing Insights*, In Press.

Marques, C. S., Santos, G., Ratten, V. and Barros, A. B. (2019) 'Innovation as a booster of rural artisan entrepreneurship: A case study of black pottery', *International Journal of Entrepreneurial Behavior & Research*, 25(4): 753–772.

Martins, E. and Terblanche, F. (2003) 'Building organizational culture that stimulates creativity and innovation', *European Journal of Innovation Management*, 16(1): 64–74.

Parnell, D., Widdop, P., Bond, A. and Wilson, R. (2020) 'Covid-19, networks and sport', *Managing Sport and Leisure*, In Press.

Ratten, V. and Braga, V. (2019) 'Tourism innovation', *Journal of Tourism and Hospitality Management*, 41: 171–174.

Ratten, V. and Jones, P. (2020) 'New challenges in sport entrepreneurship for value creation', *International Entrepreneurship and Management Journal*, 16(3): 961–980.

Rodriguez-Sanchez, I., Williams, A. and Brotons, M. (2019) 'The innovation journey of new-to-tourism entrepreneurs', *Current Issues in Tourism*, 22(8): 877–904.

Santos, G., Marques, C. S. and Ratten, V. (2019) 'Entrepreneurial women's networks: The case of D'Uva – Portugal wine girls', *International Journal of Entrepreneurial Behavior & Research*, 25(2): 298–322.

Sarri, K. and Trihopoulou, A. (2005) 'Female entrepreneurs' personal characteristics and motivations: A review of the Greek situation', *Women in Management Review*, 20(1): 24–36.

Scase, R. (2012) 'The role of small businesses in the economic transformation of Eastern Europe: Real but relatively unimportant?', *International Small Business Journal*, 16(1): 13–21.

Sheth, J. (2020) 'Business of business is more than business: Managing during the Covid crisis', *Industrial Marketing Management*, 88: 261–264.

Weick, K. E. and Sutcliffe, K. M. (2011). *Managing the unexpected: Resilient performance in an age of uncertainty* (Vol. 8). New York: John Wiley & Sons.

Wenzel, M., Stanske, S. and Lieberman, M. (2020) 'Strategic responses to crisis', *Strategic Management Journal*, In Press.

Williams, T. A., Gruber, D. A., Sutcliffe, K. M., Shepherd, D. A. and Zhao, E. Y. (2017) 'Organizational response to adversity: Fusing crisis management and resilience research streams', *Academy of Management Annals*, 11(2): 733–769.

World Health Organization (2020) *Who, Coronavirus disease (Covid-19) outbreak*, www.who.int/emergencies/diseases/novel-coronavirus-2019.

2 Open innovation ecosystems during the COVID-19 pandemic

Vanessa Ratten and Clare D'Souza

Introduction

The World Health Organization declared COVID-19 a pandemic on March 11, 2020. In December 2019, COVID-19 was first detected in Wuhan, China, and initially COVID-19 was reported as a new type of coronavirus that then spread to other parts of the world. COVID-19 has caused widespread havoc in the global economy due to the concurrent health, society, and economic problems it has caused. Some sectors of the economy such as hospitality and tourism have been affected more than others due to travel restrictions and social distancing requirements. The impact of COVID-19 is unprecedented as never before has an epidemic had such an effect on the global economy. While there have been previous epidemics, COVID-19 has caused more technological changes than others. This is due to the reduced physical contact in society requiring communication through technological devices.

COVID-19 is a highly contagious disease with no known specific cures or vaccines. This means nonmedical interventions such as social distancing have been implemented in order to decrease transmission rates. This has decreased person-to-person contact and increased reliance on technological devices for communication. As a result, there has been an upsurge in digital technology usage particularly through computer-to-human interaction. This has meant an increased interest in artificial intelligence and robotic technology. The benefit of robots is that they can provide contactless service and replace human-to-human contact services. Prior to COVID-19, the tourism industry has experienced a long period of growth characterized by the introduction of the term 'over-tourism' being used. This completely changed with COVID-19 as travel being significantly curtailed and physical movement restricted. Moreover, businesses can no longer operate alone during the COVID-19 pandemic as they require other businesses either as suppliers or as customers to survive. Thus, increasingly businesses are realizing that cooperation networks that incorporate others in their value chain are beneficial.

The purpose of this chapter is to review the current state of knowledge about open innovation by focusing on the role of social forms of cooperation. The current literature on open innovation is based on understanding the process through a community model that highlights the need for stakeholder interaction. This means innovation is viewed as a collective purpose that entities of different sizes and forms can engage in. Therefore, this chapter discusses the way the term 'open innovation' can be described on the basis of the environmental context, which is particularly useful in times of crisis.

Crisis management

Crises involve an unpredicted event so there is usually not much time to prepare for their occurrence in the marketplace. Bhaduri (2019) suggests that crises can occur from an internal or external basis. Internal crises involve some kind of unanticipated change within an organization. This can include changes in leadership, unexpected financial events, and ethical failures. Internal crisis means they are normally restricted to one organization so the impact is restricted to the stakeholders related to the organization (Comfort, 2007). External crises involve events that impact a number of organizations. COVID-19 is an external crisis that has impacted global society in an unprecedented way.

Pearson and Mitroff (1993) suggest that a crisis involves five main stages: signal detection, preparation/prevention, containment/damage limitation, recovery, and learning. In the case of COVID-19, the initial outbreak in China was contained through lockdown measures. This then made other countries try to prevent the spread of the disease through border closures. Unfortunately, this did not work as the virus spread to other countries. As a result, containment strategies were enacted, which tried to mitigate the spread of the virus. This not only limited the potential social damages but also inflicted other forms of hardship. As the COVID-19 pandemic is currently ongoing, there are some attempts to look beyond the pandemic, but there is still much uncertainty as to how that will progress. This means it is important for society to learn about COVID-19 and to derive new strategies to ensure future crises and catastrophes are handled in the right way.

Unexpected catastrophes such as epidemics, natural disasters, and economic collapses each cause different types of change. Epidemics are harder to predict and plan for due to their unknown origin. Natural disasters occur on a more common basis and there are risk management strategies in place to deal with them. Economic collapses typically occur on the basis of changes in politics.

Managing crises in the form of emergencies centers around communication, coordination, and control (Comfort, 2007). Communication can occur in written or verbal format. It is important to communicate constantly new and relevant information about COVID-19. This enables individuals to coordinate their activities and to better control outbreaks. To do this, some degree of cognition is required. Cognition is defined as 'the capacity to recognise the degree of emerging risk to which a community is exposed and to act on that information' (Comfort, 2007:189). Individuals who utilize their cognition can better manage COVID-19 and potential changes.

The COVID-19 pandemic has resulted in unprecedented change that has affected all sectors of the economy. The spread of COVID-19 in China affected economic activities which then had spillover consequences for other countries. As China is among the world's largest producers and exporters, the economic flow on effects to other countries has been significant. The economic impact can be seen in reduced manufacturing capabilities and restrictions on international mobility. Social effects in terms of closure of schools, universities, and workplaces led to an increase in online working and learning. The Spanish flu of 1911–1912 was the most similar pandemic in terms of impact. While there have been other pandemics, the impact of the COVID-19 pandemic has been more severe. During the pandemic, many individuals have shifted to working from home and this societal change may continue in the future. After the pandemic passes, it is expected that individuals will continue working from home and more businesses will have working from home models to facilitate knowledge sharing.

Knowledge

Knowledge is defined as 'a fluid mix of framed experience, values, contextual information, and expert insights that provides a framework for evaluating and incorporating new experiences and information' (Davenport and Prusak, 1998:5). In order to acquire information about emerging technologies, firms are increasingly relying on obtaining external knowledge that can be added to their existing knowledge base. This process of knowledge acquisition involves utilizing the inflow and outflow of knowledge for competitiveness reasons. Increasingly knowledge is being considered as a strategic asset that differentiates well-performing firms from nonperforming firms (Duran-Sanchez, Ratten, Del Rio Rama and Alvarez-Garcia, 2019). For this reason, innovation often results from the use of knowledge for strategic purposes. While not all knowledge is useful for innovation, certain forms of knowledge are more relevant than others. This includes knowledge about new business practices that can result in game-changing ideas in the global marketplace. Research and development (R&D) capabilities in firms rely on the continual flow of knowledge for scientific discoveries. Knowledge that is exchanged across different settings can result in collaborative production taking place (Ferreira, Fernandes and Ratten, 2019).

Knowledge is a source of intelligence for those who obtain and utilize it in the right way. While knowledge exists in many different forms and sources, obtaining the right kind of knowledge can be difficult. In addition, many firms and individuals are competing for knowledge so the process of acquiring good types of knowledge is important (Galvao, Mascarenhas, Marques, Ferreira and Ratten, 2019). Knowledge can be freely available or difficult to obtain due to confidentiality and intellectual property concerns. This means R&D collaborations might stress the kind of knowledge being shared and have associated intellectual property protocols to protect it. As a result of the trade-off being made between sharing knowledge while protecting its sources of origin, many tensions result. This means there is a paradox of wanting to share knowledge but also protecting it for competitive reasons.

Under conditions of change and market turmoil, it is useful to strategically reposition knowledge. This can be done by specifying which entities can access the knowledge, then facilitating interfirm networks to obtain timely information updates about the knowledge. Interfirm networks provide a way for firms to adjust quickly to new strategic opportunities by accessing, which requires knowledge sources (Gëerguri-Rashiti, Ramadani, Abazi-Alili, Dana and Ratten, 2017). The search for novel knowledge is considered a process involving exploring new possibilities. This means considering alternative sources of action as a way to induce the flow of knowledge. Knowledge from existing sources can be applied in new ways that involve a process of exploitation. Knowledge sharing is a good way of making available existing sources of information (Jones, Klapper, Ratten and Fayolle, 2018). However, it does not create an obligation of reciprocal knowledge exchange that results in innovation.

Innovation

Innovation involves creating something new (Potts and Ratten, 2016). This broad definition of innovation can be further refined by examining specific types of innovation such as product, process, marketing, supply, and organizational. Product innovation involves change involving a tangible resource. This means new or improved methods of production are integrated into a product. Process innovation involves changes in the way things are done. This intangible change includes introducing new ways of behaving. Marketing innovation involves developing new communication methods that often take into account technological innovation. Supply innovation refers to developing new supply markets that integrate emerging production methods. Organizational innovation refers to a change in the way an entity conducts itself (Ratten, 2018). This can include reorganization or restructuring of existing processes.

Innovation is a key ingredient of economic change and influences the productivity rate of entities within society. In an increasingly competitive environment, innovation provides a way for existing firms to maintain their market position and for new entrants to obtain market entry. Innovation can result in small changes that do not end in market disruption but rather act as improvement mechanisms. These minor changes are referred to as incremental innovation due to the change building on existing capabilities. This enables existing innovations to be improved on the basis of feedback. Incremental innovation is necessary in society as a form of continual improvement. In addition, as innovations become more widely used in society it can help to make improvements that enable better functionality. Radical innovations result in bigger changes and produce more disruption in society. Typically revolutionary products and services that involve technological innovation are referred to as being radical forms of innovation.

Innovation as a word has a variety of meanings, depending on its context. Innovation can be conceptualized as a change that incorporates some sense of novelty. The degree of this novelty can be small or large, depending on the type of change. Most forms of innovation involve some degree of interactivity between the producer of the innovation and the user of the innovation. This means the end user of a product or service is an important part of the innovation process. Innovations that have a high level of uncertainty required the help and feedback given by users for improvement reasons. Innovation can be defined in a more narrow sense as 'the implementation of a new or improved product or process and a new marketing or organizational methods in intercompany operations, workplace, organization and business relations' (Simao and Franco, 2018:3). This definition implies that there is an abundance of research focusing on different aspects of innovation due to the increased usages of innovation in everyday life. This has meant other types of change that have a non-innovation type have been neglected. Innovation is a dynamic capability as it is based on patterns of thinking that result in change. This means innovation is a way of improving the effectiveness of a product, service, or process. Innovation is associated with creative thinking due to the way some form of action leads to improvements in performance.

Innovation consists of two main stages: initiation and implementation (Harding, Lock and Toohey, 2016). The initiation stage involves introducing a new way of thinking or product into the marketplace. This can be a difficult step due to the need to get consumers interested in the innovation. For this reason, it is helpful to stress the positive advantages of the innovation in terms of its usefulness. This might also involve highlighting how the innovation can be integrated into existing processes. The implementation stage refers to how the innovation is adopted by users. This involves assessing how the innovation can be introduced into existing practices. The implementation of an innovation will be influenced by its perceived novelty in relation to the status quo. This means more consumers will be less receptive to radical innovations unless they can see the advantages. Moreover, radical innovations will result in major changes to current processes; this means a greater proportion of entities in a community will be affected by the innovation.

The design process model of business model innovation consists of five stages: observe, synthesize, generate, refine, and implement (Zott and Amit, 2010). Observe means examining how consumers currently use products and services. This means personally viewing the process rather than relying on second-hand sources. Observation is useful in gaining a better understanding about how businesses work in the marketplace. Noticing how things are occurring brings a better sense of understanding about the topic. This enables more details to be ascertained about how things are occurring in practice. To do this, observation techniques that help to understand the process are needed. This includes following customers and then asking them questions about their behavior. Thereby helping to bring a better understanding of what is occurring in a real-time format. Visual techniques such as photographs or videos can also be useful in understanding how things occur. In addition, customers can be asked to map out the process to understand the steps taken. The focus should be on all types of interaction that a customer has with a business from the initial discussion about a product to the after-sales service. This will enable information to be obtained on the role different stakeholders play in a business. The observation stage is complex as there are numerous ways to conduct this stage based on the priorities of the observer. To fully understand a business, care needs to be taken during this stage.

The synthesize stage involves taking into account everything that has been learnt during the observation stage. This means carefully considering the information and then sharing the information that has been acquired. To do this, the data need to be analyzed in terms of assessing potential patterns. This will enable a better understanding of why things occur like they do in the marketplace. By identifying key themes and issues in the data, a holistic understanding about the business is obtained. This will enable patterns of behavior to emerge based on the events occurring in the marketplace. Extracting information from the data can take time especially if the information is hard to understand. This means using techniques such as mind mapping to analyze linkages between themes.

Generate means creating potential solutions to problems. This can occur through a creative path that enables different ideas to be brainstormed. The generation of ideas is best done in practice to see how potential solutions can be implemented. In order to generate ideas, it helps to have the feedback from others to reassess possibilities. This enables individuals to build on the ideas of others to obtain better outcomes. By encouraging the flow of information to disseminate between individuals, more comprehensive ideas can emerge. In order to obtain the best ideas, it is useful to encourage daydreaming. This enables individuals freedom to think in a different manner than they normally would. Innovation often occurs through deliberate action but can also occur via serendipity. This means how we think about innovation is influenced by input from others. Daydreaming can enable an individual to pursue new possibilities that previously were not considered. To do this properly, individuals need to think about ideas in a novel way. This can lead to the creation of entirely new systems unleashed by a flow of creativity so it is important to keep in mind that ideas are generated in different ways.

The refine process involves narrowing down potential possibilities in a more detailed way. This involves choosing the best ideas and then evaluating them based on set criteria. To do this, solutions should be discussed with stakeholders through both formal and informal communication. The refinement of ideas does not have to be in a deliberate manner but can also occur in an ad hoc fashion. Although the use of a dedicated team to concept test ideas can help. It can help to prototype or test ideas to see which one works. To do this, suggested ideas need to be circulated to develop rapid prototyping. This would give an idea a more tangible nature and allow others to try it. By identifying the strengths and weaknesses of the idea, it can lead to further improvements. The prototyping can involve a set of interactive activities that are conducted to see how realistic the idea is in the marketplace. This will give life to ideas and enable a better understanding of potential solutions. By exploring multiple direction an idea can take, it will hopefully lead to more successful outcomes. Part of this process involves presenting prototypes to stakeholders in order to gauge their reaction. Based on feedback, the idea is then further refined. To do this, different viewpoints are consolidated to make the changes. The implement stage means advancing the idea into the marketplace to others who can use it. This means making necessary adaptations to existing processes to smooth the process. Some modifications may need to be made to better fit the requirements of the market. Not all ideas can be implemented quickly as some changes will need to occur. This means the implementation of an idea may occur over an extended period of time.

Innovation processes have accelerated due to the ongoing increase in the knowledge economy. The global availability of knowledge has meant an increase in the way knowledge is utilized for economic success. Moreover, shorter innovation cycles have meant a reliance on continued knowledge acquisition. In order to seek new opportunities for commercialization, there needs to be further focus on knowledge management. This enables traditional business models to change to a more open environment in which knowledge is more freely circulated.

Rogers (1983) suggests that the likely success of an innovation is based on five attributes: (1) relative advantage, (2) compatibility, (3) trialability, (4) observability, and (5) complexity. The relative advantage refers to the degree of newness or difference between prior innovations and the current innovation. Innovations that are perceived as useful are likely to be more successful. However, an innovation also needs to be easy to use in order for it to gain market acceptance. Compatibility refers to how the innovation fits into current market practices. Innovations that supersede previous practices need to still align with current market conditions. This means analyzing the needs of potential adopters to see how the innovation fits into their lifestyle. The degree of fit between past and current experiences also needs to align with existing market practices. Trialability refers to how individuals utilize and innovation and whether further iterations are required to increase its appeal in the market. This can involve testing and prototyping different ideas to improve performance. Observability of results means understanding how the innovation is being adopted in society. Sometimes the original innovation might not be used in the same way that it was conceived. Complexity involves how difficult it is to understand an innovation. Opportunities can be discovered by being alert to unmet needs. This involves entrepreneurs focusing on what current problems are not being addressed in society. This process involves acquiring knowledge about current market practices and then forecasting potential need. In order to recognize certain opportunities, it can help to have a systematic search process. This involves discovering opportunities based on a search of current needs. Doing this helps to have entrepreneurs interact with others in the market to create social forms of innovation.

Social innovation

Social innovation differs from traditional types of innovation by focusing on more community type of activities. This means the focus is on the habitat and health of individuals within a community setting. Governments are spending more money on the nonprofit and social sector due to demands from the community. While some social services can be outsourced, in times of a crisis like COVID-19, governments need to prioritize social services. Social innovation is a difficult phenomenon to describe due to its definition changing based on the environmental conditions. For some, social innovation can be quick as it results in a positive change in society. For others, social innovation is a long and complex event that is difficult to predict. This means it can be complex to understand the nature and origins of social innovation unless it is considered in conjunction with the environmental context. Social innovation is generally referred to as the implementation of new ideas within an existing social system. This highlights the need to generate new ideas based on human needs.

Additional attention is clearly needed to understand how to identify ways to support and encourage entrepreneurship during the COVID-19 pandemic. Social innovation provides a way to respond to unsolved social needs that have been unsuccessfully addressed in the marketplace. Due to the COVID-19 pandemic, there has been an increase in social problems that cannot be solved by the government. Therefore, more social innovation is required to identify and implement new services that improve the quality of life for society. Social innovation fills gaps in society that neither the private sector nor the government can fill.

Social innovation can be defined as 'a novel solution to a social problem that is more effective, efficient, or just than existing solutions and for which the value created accrues primarily to society as a whole rather than private individuals' (Phills, Deiglmeier and Miller, 2008:39). The concept of social innovation is particularly needed during the COVID-19 crisis due to the profound social shifts that have occurred. Social innovation helps to address unmet social needs through societal action. This is due to social innovation embedding a stakeholder orientation to finding solutions to problems that rely on a number of stakeholders for input.

Open innovation

Closed innovation normally refers to in-house exploitation and/or distribution (Inauen and Schenker-Wicki, 2012). This means the innovation is only known to those inside an organization and the knowledge is not shared with others. In the past, this way was considered the best approach to managing innovation. It helped organizations gain a superior market advantage while ensuring future innovations also stayed in-house. More recently a process called inside-out open innovation has become popular due to market advantages. This means there is a potential for others to supplement or add to the existing innovation.

Examples of inside-out open innovation include licensing, open-source innovation, participating in other companies, and sale and/or divestment (Inauen and Schenker-Wicki, 2012).

External participation in open innovation strategies can lead to better industry engagement. The inside-out open innovation process is defined as 'the commercialization of ideas, technologies and innovations via external distribution channels' (Inauen and Schenker-Wicki, 2012:216). This means external sources of innovation are required to foster new ideas. Thereby outside influencers such as customers, competitors, and suppliers can produce change that then is implemented in another context. Other entities, including research institutions and universities, play a key role in sourcing new ideas and technologies. Thereby providing ideas from outside sources to be brought to the market more quickly, Enkel, Gassman and Chebrough (2009:312) refer to the inside-out process as 'earning profits by bringing ideas to market, selling intellectual property and multiplying technology by transferring ideas to the outside environment.' The notion of this inside-out process is that open innovation refers to the need to open up innovation processes to external entities to facilitate a process of co-creation. This means combining internal and external sources of innovation to create new value.

Open innovation is a popular way to foster innovation due to the increasing time-based concerns faced by many companies. This means time is a strategic weapon when utilized in the right way. The rapidly growing body of literature associated with open innovation is due to its practical significance in the global economy. In organizations there is a tendency to keep ideas in-house and not to share ideas externally. This is a natural tendency due to the need to protect current market positions. However, changing organizational cultures are valuing new ideas and are changing the current status quo. This means leadership of an organization can help facilitate more open processes in innovation.

Elmquist, Fredberg and Ollila (2009:340) describe open innovation as 'an internal process that is becoming more dependent on external knowledge and external actors, but it still considers innovation as an internal process.' Open innovation normally means that the boundaries of a firm are opened to others in order to facilitate the flow of information. There can be negative sides of open innovation as many different viewpoints are considered. This can result in an overreliance on crowd thinking rather than the advice of experts. This means ideas can be misunderstood and result in time being wasted. In addition, customer's feedback might be hard to implement due to practical limitations. Open innovation means purposively managing knowledge flows in the broader environmental context. This means the knowledge flow is not restricted to a specific organization, but rather has a free-flowing nature that combines ideas found in external entities made possible through coopetition.

Coopetition

Coopetition is a way organizations can gain access to innovation. Brandenburger and Nalebuff (1996) introduced the concept of coopetition to a business audience. In the quick-changing business environment, coopetition provides a way for businesses to compete with each other but also cooperate on projects. Bouncken, Gast, Kraus and Bogers (2015:591) define coopetition as 'a strategic and dynamic process in which economic actors jointly create value through cooperative interaction, while they simultaneously compete to capture part of that value.' This definition implies that collaborating while competing provides a way for organizations to obtain useful information that can be beneficial for performance results.

Coopetition is useful when each organization has something to offer that can collectively lead to better outcomes. This means that coopetition can provide a way to obtain resources that would otherwise be hard to obtain. The main benefits of coopetition include 'the exchange of resources, capabilities and knowledge' (Hora, Gast, Kailer, Rey-Marti and Mas-Tur et al, 2018:414). Coopetition enables organizations to simultaneously cooperate and compete, thereby facilitating mutual needs. The main reasons for coopetition arise from the way organizations can pool their resources and knowledge to promote innovation. This strategy facilitates new product development that is required in the ever-changing business world. The initial idea of coopetition was criticized due to a belief that competing organizations could not also collaborate. This belief changed when organizations realized that there were benefits associated with the coopetition process. Despite the positive result from coopetition, there are still risks that can result in failure. This means the general belief about coopetition needs to be mitigated by potential risks.

One way of dealing with the pressure of change is to collaborate with other businesses to develop new products. More businesses are incorporating collaborative agreements into their product portfolios as a way to generate new ideas. This collaborative process enables businesses to construct a network of businesses that can help them develop a wide variety of products over a longer period of time. Innovation networks are particularly important in the COVID-19 environment where changes occur rapidly and there is a need to respond to consumer demands in a short time period. New ideas often arise from collaboration with others since these businesses give access to a different knowledge base. Businesses establish relationships with other businesses that they infrequently interact with, which are called weak tie partnerships (Dittrich and Duysters, 2007). These kinds of partnerships enable businesses to benefit from resources outside of their normal industry. Weak tie partnerships are characterized by a lower level of commitment to sharing ideas about new projects.

Co-creation is a new way of thinking about the benefits of participation from multiple stakeholders that are evident in the process of coopetition. Co-creation enables stakeholders to offer suggestions and input on entrepreneurial activity. Individuals are linked through social interaction, so co-creation is a natural progression. Co-creation merges both social and communication processes in order to derive mutual gain. It is useful to have input from others rather than relying on one individual. Co-creation does not necessarily mean creating a new business venture as it can also involve shared interpretation. This means individuals through interactions can share a common understanding about meanings. The nature of co-creation depends on the environmental context. This means in times of crisis such as the COVID-19 pandemic, the type of co-creation will involve ideas related more to technological innovation. Other types of co-creation may also occur depending on the goal of the collaboration process. The main reward for participating in co-creation is the intrinsic benefit received by the individual.

Inherent in the concept of co-creation is an assumption that innovation will occur. This means co-creation normally involves creating more relevant things or processes. This contrasts to a traditional stage-gate research and development process that limits the involvement of outsiders. Co-creation implies that individuals within an organization share knowledge with those outside the organization. The idea behind co-creation is that through the participation of users, a better idea will result. Involving users from the initial idea stage through to the commercialization stage can save time and money. This enables the co-creation process to overcome potential problems before they occur in the marketplace. In addition, the actual needs of the users instead of the perceived needs are considered. Active user involvement enables user scenarios to be considered. This enables the idea to be better tailored for consumers and facilitates an ecosystem approach to the sharing of knowledge.

Ecosystems

The main type of ecosystems is business, innovation, and entrepreneurial (Hakala, O'Shea, Farny and Luoto, 2019). Business ecosystems focus more on the evolution of businesses into entities that require some form of coopetition. Coopetition occurs when businesses collaborate and compete in order to realize market synergies. Due to the changing circumstances of many businesses, a global approach to market selection is required (Abazi-Alili, Ramadani, Ratten, Abazi-Caushi and Rexhepi, 2016). This enables businesses to realize they are part of a system based on connections. In order to improve value in a business, there needs to be some form of leadership through coopetition. This enables the ecosystem to be governed by those interested in facilitating its growth. In a business ecosystem, not all entities are equal as there will be winners and losers in each market transaction. This makes strategy a necessity for competition in order to realize positive results. Within the business ecosystem, there will be some entities that are stronger and have more power because of their market position. This makes the leading businesses need to support new businesses in order to progress the ecosystem.

Innovation ecosystems differ from business ecosystems due to the emphasis on co-creation. This means unlike business ecosystems that emphasize competition as well as cooperation, innovation ecosystems rely on value derived from collaborating on projects (Coelho, Marques, Loureiro and Ratten, 2018). In this sense, the innovation provides a source of cohesion among the ecosystem members. This means that entities in an innovation ecosystem realize the need for complementary entities. By focusing on key innovative projects, entities can integrate their research and development efforts. This enables entities to be connected to others outside of their organization.

Entrepreneurial ecosystems differ again to innovation and business forms of ecosystems by stressing the role of policy in business decisions (Ratten, 2017). This means the emphasis is on regions in terms of how multiple stakeholders interact in order to contribute to a systemic flow of knowledge emphasizing entrepreneurial endeavors (Ratten, 2019). There are different components required in an entrepreneurial ecosystem in order for it to function properly. This includes entrepreneurs, investors, government bodies, policy makers, and the community. Regional actors realize that entrepreneurship often needs to be considered as a collective effort based on an innovative mindset. This means regions can encourage others to act in an entrepreneurial manner (Ratten, Ferreira and Fernandes, 2016).

Audretsch, Cunningham, Kuratko, Lehmann and Menter (2019) refer to entrepreneurial ecosystems having an economic, societal, and technological impact. The economic aspect relates to the financial or productive outcomes from the collaboration while the social aspect implies information dissemination. The technological aspect focuses more on innovation that is derived from an integration of network members. Within an ecosystem, there needs to be some degree of coherence in the goals, activities, and values. This helps to produce a more vibrant entrepreneurial ecosystem due to the existence of collective norms. An entrepreneurial ecosystem aims to foster entrepreneurial activity within a given area (Ratten and Tajeddini, 2017). This means it tends to refer to a generic context that is based on network interactions. Networks can be horizontal in terms of competitors or vertical in terms of the supply chain. The entities in an entrepreneurial ecosystem are based on the idea that frequent and collaborative interaction is required to produce entrepreneurial ideas (Ratten et al., 2016). This means entrepreneurs are supported by funding agencies, government entities, and customers in their ability to produce certain products or services. Not all entities in an ecosystem are the same as they depend upon the active participation of businesses and trade associations. Stam (2015) suggested that an entrepreneurial ecosystem comprises framework and systemic conditions. Framework conditions include culture, demand, infrastructure, and institutions (Qian, 2018). Systemic conditions involve finance, knowledge, leadership, networks, support services, and talent (Qian, 2018).

Conclusion

This chapter has focused on how the COVID-19 pandemic in the form of a crisis requires an open innovation approach to knowledge sharing. This means harnessing the collective potential of a group of entities to enable market solutions to be derived. To do this, it is useful to highlight the way social innovation is needed that enables different entities to collaborate but also compete. This process is referred to as coopetition and was discussed in this chapter as a positive way to facilitate change. This is useful in the COVID-19 pandemic that needs open innovation in the form of ecosystems in order to encourage knowledge exchange.

References

Abazi-Alili, H., Ramadani, V., Ratten, V., Abazi-Caushi, B. and Rexhepi, G. (2016) 'Encouragement factors of social entrepreneurial activities in Europe', *International Journal of Foresight and Innovation Policy*, 11(4): 225–239.

Audretsch, D. B., Cunningham, J. A., Kuratko, D. F., Lehmann, E. E. and Menter, M. (2019) 'Entrepreneurial ecosystems: economic, technological, and societal impacts', *The Journal of Technology Transfer*, 44(2): 313–325.

Bhaduri, R. M. (2019) 'Leveraging culture and leadership in crisis management', *European Journal of Training and Development*, 43(5/6): 554–569.

Bouncken, R., Gast, J., Kraus, S. and Bogers, M. (2015) 'Coopetition: A review, synthesis and future research directions', *Review of Managerial Science*, 9(3): 577–601.

Brandenburger, A. and Nalebuff, B. (1996) *Co-opetition*. New York: Doubleday.

Coelho, F. J. M., Marques, C., Loureiro, A. and Ratten, V. (2018) 'Evaluation of the impact of an entrepreneurship training program in Recife, Brazil', *Journal of Entrepreneurship in Emerging Economies*, 10(3): 472–488.

Comfort, L. K. (2007) 'Crisis management in hindsight: Cognition, communication, coordination, and control', *Public Administration Review*, 67: 189–197.

Davenport, T. H. and Prusak, L. (1998) *Working knowledge: How organizations manage what they know*. Cambridge, MA: Harvard Business Press.

Dittrich, K. and Duysters, G. (2007) 'Networking as a means to strategy change: The case of open innovation in mobile telephony', *Journal of Product Innovation Management*, 24(6): 510–521.

Duran-Sanchez, A., Ratten, V., Del Rio Rama, M. and Alvarez-Garcia, J. (2019) 'Trends and changes in the *International Journal of Entrepreneurial Behaviour & Research*: A bibliometric review', *International Journal of Entrepreneurial Behaviour & Research*, 25(7): 1494–1514.

Elmquist, M., Fredberg, T. and Ollila, S. (2009) 'Exploring the field of open innovation', *European Journal of Innovation Management*, 12(3): 326–345.

Enkel, E., Gassman, O. and Chebrough, H. (2009) 'Open R&D and open innovation: Exploring the phenomenon', *R&D Management*, 39(4): 311–316.

Ferreira, J. J., Fernandes, C. and Ratten, V. (2019) 'The effects of technology transfers and institutional factors on economic growth: Evidence from Europe and Oceania', *The Journal of Technology Transfer*, 44(5): 1505–1528.

Galvao, A., Mascarenhas, C., Marques, C., Ferreira, J. and Ratten, V. (2019) 'Triple helix and its evolution: A systematic literature review', *Journal of Science and Technology Policy*, 10(3): 812–833.

Gërguri-Rashiti, S., Ramadani, V., Abazi-Alili, H., Dana, L.-P. and Ratten, V. (2017) 'ICT, innovation and firm performance: The transition economies context', *Thunderbird International Business Review*, 59(1): 93–102.

Hakala, H., O'Shea, G., Farny, S. and Luoto, S. (2019) 'Re-storying the business, innovation and entrepreneurial ecosystem concepts: The model-narrative review method', *International Journal of Management Reviews*, 1–23.

Harding, J., Lock, D. and Toohey, K. (2016) 'A social identity analysis of technological innovation in an action sport: Judging elite half-pipe snowboarding', *European Sport Management Quarterly*, 16(2): 214–232.

Hora, W., Gast, J., Kailer, N., Rey-Marti, A. and Mas-Tur, A. (2018) 'David and Goliath: Causes and effects of coopetition between start-ups and corporates', *Review of Managerial Science*, 12: 411–439.

Inauen, M. and Schenker-Wicki, A. (2012) 'Fostering radical innovations with open innovation', *European Journal of Innovation Management*, 15(2): 212–231.

Jones, P., Klapper, R., Ratten, V. and Fayolle, A. (2018) 'Emerging themes in entrepreneurial behaviours, identities and contexts', *International Journal of Entrepreneurship and Innovation*, 19(4): 233–236.

Pearson, C. M. and Mitroff, I. I. (1993) 'From crisis prone to crisis prepared: A framework for crisis management', *Academy of Management Perspectives*, 7(1): 48–59.

Phills, J. A., Deiglmeier, K. and Miller, D. T. (2008) 'Rediscovering social innovation', *Stanford Social Innovation Review*, 6(4): 34–43.

Potts, J. and Ratten, V. (2016) 'Sports innovation: Introduction to the Special section', *Innovation Management, Policy & Practice*, 18(3): 233–237.

Qian, H. (2018) 'Knowledge-based regional economic development: A synthetic review of knowledge spillovers, entrepreneurship, and entrepreneurial ecosystems', *Economic Development Quarterly*, 32(2): 163–176.

Ratten, V. (2017) 'Gender entrepreneurship and global marketing', *Journal of Global Marketing*, 30(3): 114–121.

Ratten, V. (2018) 'Social entrepreneurship through digital communication in farming', *World Journal of Entrepreneurship, Management and Sustainable Development*, 14(1): 99–110.

Ratten, V. (2019) 'Understanding the emergence of sport entrepreneurship: Policy considerations and agenda setting', *Journal of Entrepreneurship and Public Policy*, 8(1): 1–4.

Ratten, V., Ferreira, J. and Fernandes, C. (2016) 'Entrepreneurial and network knowledge in emerging economies', *Review of International Business and Strategy*, 26(3): 392–409.

Ratten, V. and Tajeddini, K. (2017) 'Women's entrepreneurship and internationalization: Patterns and trends', *International Journal of Sociology and Social Policy*, 38(9/10): 780–793.

Rogers, E. M. (1983) *Diffusion of Innovations*, 3rd ed. New York: The Free Press.

Simao, L. and Franco, M. (2018) 'External knowledge sources as antecedents of organizational innovation in firm workplaces: A knowledge-based perspective', *Journal of Knowledge Management*, 22(2): 237–256.

Stam, E. (2015) 'Entrepreneurial ecosystems and regional policy: A sympathetic critique', *European Planning Studies*, 23(9): 1759–1769.

Zott, C. and Amit, R. (2010) 'Business model design: An activity system perspective', *Long Range Planning*, 43(2–3): 216–226.

3 Small business risk and entrepreneurship during the COVID-19 pandemic

Vanessa Ratten

Introduction

Small businesses are of great benefit to society due to the positive externalities they produce (Lewis and Churchill, 1983). This includes social cohesion and access to needed services in a community. The COVID-19 pandemic has created new challenges for small businesses in terms of cashflow, workplace practices, and supply chain issues. As a result, many small businesses are experiencing severe hardship as a result of the COVID-19 pandemic, while some are facing surprising gains. The mixture of positive and negative effects of the COVID-19 pandemic on small businesses means it is important that they can react flexibly to challenges in a positive way. To do this, small businesses need to demonstrate great entrepreneurial flexibility in how they handle the challenges associated with the COVID-19 pandemic. This means focusing on learning effects that have occurred and trying to develop new knowledge.

Small businesses that rely on high levels of human interaction have been greatly affected by COVID-19. This means there are multiple interpretations of risk with most referring to unintended outcomes derived from human contact. Risks can be considered as things that prevent perfect outcomes from occurring (Ratten and Dana, 2017). In order to minimize risk, cooperative entrepreneurship is required in the COVID-19 pandemic due to the need for multiple entities to work together for social gain. Cooperative entrepreneurship differs from other forms of entrepreneurship by emphasizing collective wealth (Ratten, 2016). This means unlike traditional entrepreneurship that emphasizes individual goals, in cooperative entrepreneurship, the focus is on co-creation. There can be different reasons for co-creation including the exchange of knowledge and technology, which helps to reduce costs by sharing resources (Ratten, Ferreira and Fernandes, 2017). Moreover, the main incentive for cooperation is to obtain a competitive advantage in the marketplace.

Currently, there are few studies that have dealt with the effects of the COVID-19 pandemic on small businesses in terms of cooperative entrepreneurship and risk management. While much practical evidence exists about the effects, few academic studies have occurred. This may be due to the recent and ongoing nature of the crisis. With respect to this temporary gap in the literature, this chapter fills this gap by focusing on emerging practices. Thus, this chapter explores the most important aspects of COVID-19 for small businesses. To this end, the influence of COVID-19 on small business will be discussed from a number of perspectives. The general and financial implications are stated but special attention is paid to the role of small businesses in the global economy. The consequences of COVID-19 on small businesses will be analyzed. This will include a discussion on the role of government policy and society in helping small businesses adjust to the new conditions. Overall, the chapter emphasizes in a different way how small businesses have been affected by COVID-19. This is important as small businesses have specific differences to large businesses that merit a different kind of analysis. Therefore, this chapter takes a fresh approach to inquiring how small business is affected by COVID-19. This is a timely and highly relevant topic given the significant impact COVID-19 has had on the global economy.

COVID-19 crisis

COVID-19 has caused the first major pandemic of the twenty-first century that most likely will surpass previous pandemics in terms of its effect on society. Amoros (2020:337) states 'on 30 January 2020, the World Health Organisation, WHO, declared the COVID-19 outbreak as the sixth public health emergency of international concern after 2003 SARS-CoV crisis: H1N1 (2009). Polio (2014), Ebola in West Africa (2014), Zika (2016) and Ebola in the Democratic Republic of Congo (2019).' There were previously warning signs that a health pandemic would occur, but most governments considered themselves ready to deal with potential outbreaks. The COVID-19 pandemic has shown that a health pandemic can cause large economic and social effects. The current COVID-19 pandemic has spread globally with both developed and developing countries affected in the same way. This is due to society being highly mobile and internationally connected (Walker, Holling, Carpenter and Kinzig, 2004). Despite significant health improvements in the past 100 years, the current COVID-19 pandemic is being treated with preventions like social distancing and isolation that were used during the 1918 Spanish flu pandemic.

The stark inequalities between small and large businesses have been laid bare by the COVID-19 crisis. Small businesses that rely on a constant cash flow have seen massive shifts in their financial position. This has resulted in a downturn in their normal operating position. Large businesses on the other hand typically have some form of financial reserve that provides a buffer in times of crises. Some large businesses have more financial reserves than others so normally each business needs to be considered on the basis of their circumstances. The COVID-19 pandemic has caused many small businesses to close down or limit their hours of operation. This has caused a societal problem due to the social consequences of altered business practices. It is important that small businesses involved in the crisis take the time to reflect and strategize for the future. In this way, small businesses can see the crisis as a form of hardship but also as a source of opportunity. Moreover, the interplay between business and society is evident in the COVID-19 crisis. This has meant a struggle between economic and social ramifications from the COVID-19 crisis.

The COVID-19 pandemic has awakened people's awareness of the inequalities in society. Preventive measures such as social distancing and lockdowns are only available to those who can afford to do so (Bapuji, Patel, Ertug and Allen, 2020). This has meant most affluent or wealthy societies have been able to decrease the spread of the virus due to non-pharmacological interventions. Moreover, individuals needing to quarantine should have the financial reserves to do this although some governments have subsidized the quarantine period. However, some developing and emerging economies have also had success in combating the virus despite being in a weaker financial position. For example, Thailand and Vietnam have had relatively low rates of infection compared to other countries. This difference some suggest is due to their knowledge about how to handle previous coronaviruses such as the Avian flu and Middle East Respiratory Virus (MERS). As they had skills in contact tracing and testing capabilities, they were able to decrease the level of infections in their countries.

The effect of the COVID-19 pandemic on the workforce can be understood in terms of the types of jobs people hold. Bapuji et al. (2020) suggest that jobs affected by the COVID-19 pandemic can be analyzed in terms of these categories: elite, frontline, outsourced, and the gig economy. Elite workers are in essential industries and are likely to be less affected. Frontline workers deal directly with COVID-19 patients, while outsourced workers handle secondary tasks. The gig economy refers to individuals who have portfolio careers based on a succession of jobs.

Social distancing has several adverse consequences including feelings of isolation and psychological distress. In addition, work and study configurations have had to change due to social distancing requirements. This has led to new habits being formed that change behavioral patterns. Some of these changes in terms of distancing from others are quite different from previous workplace policies that emphasized sharing. As a consequence, there has been an increase in telework and a reliance on digital technology for communication.

The COVID-19 crisis has raised debates over the need for medical intervention in the form of a cure or vaccine. As a result, there have been conflicts between countries and pharmaceutical companies about potential supplies of these products. In addition, essential supplies including face masks and hand sanitizer have become competitive items in the global marketplace. At the same time, there has been an increased emphasis on the sharing of medical information related to COVID-19. This is evident with publishers making freely available publications related to COVID-19.

Despite the emphasis on the free sharing of information and knowledge, regional trading blocs such as the European Union have drawn criticism for their response to the COVID-19 pandemic. Some European Union members closed their borders despite the Schengen agreement that relies on open border movement. Most notably Spain shut its border with neighboring countries resulting in an increase in nationalist sentiment rather than relying on regional cooperation. This is in stark contrast to previous regional policies of having open borders and increased levels of internationalization.

Despite the previous coronaviruses such as the Avian flu causing havoc many countries were unprepared for the current COVID-19 pandemic. This was surprising given the reality that it was likely that a health pandemic would occur at some time in the future. The reason for this surprise might be due to the assumption that developed countries had superior biosecurity regulations that would prevent the occurrence of a health pandemic (Adger, 2000). This assumption proved to be wrong as many developed countries around the world have had high levels of COVID-19 infections and fatalities. In some cases, the rate of infection in developed countries has been higher than that in developing countries. This unusual position has meant that COVID-19 has impacted the global economy in an unprecedented way, which necessitates the need for entrepreneurship.

Entrepreneurship

Entrepreneurship can be considered as an activity continuum with low to high levels of activity. This means there can be some confusion about the subject of entrepreneurship due to the way it is defined. Entrepreneurship can be considered as 'the capacity to perceive opportunities for change and to get things done' (Johannesson, 2012:192). This means a relational approach to understanding entrepreneurship in times of crisis is required. Baum and Locke (2004:588) consider entrepreneurs as individuals who 'discover and exploit new products, new processes, and new ways of organising.' This means that inherent in any consideration of entrepreneurs is the idea that they are doing something new. Thus, their efforts are directed at recognizing new things in the market environment. This normally involves exploiting opportunities that no one else has considered. Thus, time is of the essence in entrepreneurship as it can be used in a strategic way.

Entrepreneurship has been surfacing as a key way to deal with the changes required due to the COVID-19 pandemic. The policy and academic discourse around entrepreneurship tend to frame it in terms of economic growth. Research on entrepreneurship in the COVID-19 pandemic is relatively novel within entrepreneurship studies. This means that a relational approach to entrepreneurship during the COVID-19 pandemic is useful to understand the role of relationships in times of crisis. A relational view in which entities are part of a social network provides useful insights into the entrepreneurship process. This enables an understanding about the diverse ways entrepreneurial projects are accomplished in times of crisis.

Entrepreneurs are different from non-entrepreneurs because of their passion and emotional feelings toward business activities. Passion motivates entrepreneurs to continue their business ventures even in times of hardship. This means passion is core to entrepreneurship as it can help foster creativity. Therefore, entrepreneurs recognize new ideas that are useful in exploiting market opportunities. Entrepreneurs differ in their level of passion depending on how it is utilized as a motivational factor.

Entrepreneurial passion is defined as 'an entrepreneur intense affective state accompanied by cognitive and behavioural manifestations of high personal value' (Chen, Yao and Kotha, 2009:199). This definition recognizes that the use of emotions is important for entrepreneurs. Emotions can range from happy to being excited about possibilities in the marketplace. These emotions influence how others perceive an entrepreneur and the likelihood of its success. More passionate entrepreneurs show their feelings in verbal and nonverbal ways. This includes manifesting passion into behavioral outcomes as a way to motivate others. Entrepreneurial passion is described as 'consciously accessible intense positive feelings experienced by engagement in entrepreneurial activities associated with roles that are meaningful and salient to the self-identity of the entrepreneur' (Cardon, Wincent, Singh and Drnovsek, 2009:517). This means that passion is reflected in positive behavioral characteristics such as focusing on the benefits and advantages of business ideas. In addition, the self-identity of an entrepreneur is reflected in the way they show their feelings. This means entrepreneurs tend to have intense feelings that are evident in their communication.

The COVID-19 pandemic affected the environment in different ways, but requires the participation of individuals in order to negate its effects. Entrepreneurs' characteristics and interpersonal relationships play a key role in how society responds to the crisis. Entrepreneurs who have good relationships in the community can utilize their power in order to facilitate trust, respect, and mutual interactions. This will enhance proactive behavior in society about how to deal with the COVID-19 crisis. This will increase confidence and positively impact knowledge transfer. Entrepreneurs can utilize their social standing in society to foster relationships and impact knowledge transfer.

Entrepreneurship is a phenomenon that affects society in different ways but acts as a source of knowledge that enhances futuristic thinking. That is, entrepreneurs are most likely to develop solutions to COVID-19 problems. However, entrepreneurs during the COVID-19 crisis have different aspirations and marketing capabilities that influence their growth trajectories. Some entrepreneurs have no growth willingness that means they are not interested or available for new business opportunities. Hisrich and Peters (2002:10) define entrepreneurship as the 'process of creating something new and assuming the risks and rewards.' This implies that with any form of entrepreneurship there is potential for losses as well as gains.

Entrepreneurial opportunities

An entrepreneurial opportunity is defined as 'a set of ideas, beliefs and actions that enable the creation of future goods and services in the absence of current markets for them' (Sarasvathy, Dew, Velamuri and Venkataraman, 2003:142). The main dimensions of entrepreneurial opportunities are opportunity recognition, opportunity discovery, and opportunity creation (Edoho, 2015).

Opportunity recognition means finding a new possibility in the marketplace. In times of change, this involves acknowledging how the market environment has adapted to new societal conditions. Opportunity discovery involves finding new opportunities that have previously been neglected. This is important during the COVID-19 crisis as new ways of conducting business are required. Opportunity creation refers to integrating new thought processes into business activity. This is needed during the COVID-19 as multiple stakeholders come together in order to solve societal problems.

An entrepreneur takes responsibility for courses of action based on their assessment of the market. This means they make judgmental decisions depending on the way resources can be utilized. Entrepreneurship is a way of managing opportunities based on the resources currently available. This emphasizes the need for entrepreneurs to assemble required resources and then to start building their business venture. To do this requires a practical plan that ensures resources are used in a timely fashion. The process of entrepreneurship can be impacted by changes in demographic and social conditions. This has occurred with the COVID-19 pandemic due to the increased usage of technology by society.

In any kind of entrepreneurship, there needs to be some form of opportunity identified. This can include commercial or social opportunities depending on the context. Commercial opportunities involve the creation of financial wealth, while social opportunities refer to some kind of philanthropic or nonprofit objective. Opportunities are objective phenomena that are evaluated by an individual in terms of potential market feasibility. This means that opportunities are objects waiting to be discovered by entrepreneurs (Alvarez and Barney, 2007). As part of the discovery process, an opportunity needs to be recognized for its potential. Opportunities can also be created by entrepreneurs depending on the situation. This means the actions of an entrepreneur impact on the type of opportunities that emerge in the marketplace. Gonzalez, Husted, and Aigner (2017:213) state that opportunity discovery is 'a function of entrepreneurial alertness, based on an information search of pre-existing business solutions, the perception of the environment, and the entrepreneur's network of weak ties.' The way opportunities are discovered during the COVID-19 crisis will depend on the urgency of the solution and magnitude of the problem.

Entrepreneurs who find opportunities tend to cultivate social networks that can be sources of information. This helps to discover opportunities on the basis of actions and reactions. An entrepreneur finds ideas through acquiring knowledge. Some ideas can be more radical than others due to the extent to which the change will have an impact on society. Innovation radicalness is defined as 'a novel solution which has distinctive features that are missing in previously observed solutions, and that has a very positive impact on society and/or the environment' (Gonzalez et al., 2017:214). The process of opportunity discovery can involve innovation radicalness when it involves finding some form of idea that can lead to major change. Innovation can be incremental or radical depending on the degree of change. When the innovation results in a more positive impact, it is considered as being radical. This is due to the innovation

Table 3.1 COVID-19 innovation orientation initiatives

Focus of innovation orientation	Stakeholder orientation	Value orientation
Internally focused	Change in organizational structure based on stakeholder engagement.	Build a technologically advanced organizational system.
	Organizational processes adapted to suit new environmental conditions.	Utilize data analytics to attain economies of scale.
	Fostering an entrepreneurial culture based on stakeholder interaction.	
Externally focused	Encourage co-creation activities between customers and suppliers.	Move toward a more interactive value-based model.
	Engage in more proactive activity with stakeholders.	Experiment in developing new products and services.
	Build a digital ecosystem that enables interaction and feedback from stakeholders.	

Source: Author developed.

being perceived as highly different to existing forms of innovation. Examples of innovation orientation during the COVID-19 crisis can be considered from a stakeholder and value orientation perspective, which are stated in Table 3.1.

Workplace changes from the COVID-19 pandemic

There have been changes to job outcomes resulting from the COVID-19 pandemic. This involves the way jobs are performed on the basis of the current conditions. Many jobs are done in different circumstances due to the need for physical distancing and hygiene requirements. This has created hardship for those who also have to look after children and others when working from home. However, some individuals prefer working from home due to the flexibility it enables. This means that there can also be more suitable working conditions rather than the long commute to work previously conducted by individuals. Working from home has also raised questions about job stress and employee well-being. Due to the uncertainty of the pandemic, individuals are facing much upheaval in their lives, which is causing emotional stress.

Coping is a mechanism used by individuals in times of unknown futures. As there is currently no vaccine or cure for COVID-19, individuals have to adjust to the new conditions. This means utilizing different wellness strategies in order to create a better work/life balance. This can involve coaching or therapy designed to introduce better thought patterns. Alternatively, it can involve videoconferencing lunch breaks and meetings in order to encourage social interaction. This reduces the sense of loneliness many individuals face in the new environment. Support is required to help individuals adjust to new working and living conditions. This can occur via technology devices that mimic real-life interaction.

Venkatesh (2020) suggests that the impact of COVID-19 in jobs can be analyzed through loss, changes, outcomes, coping, and support. Job loss means that due to COVID-19 restrictions, the nature of jobs has significantly changed. High physical contact jobs such as beauty therapists and hairdressers are no longer able to perform their job in the same way. This has meant an increase in usage of personal equipment. However, the shift to a digital economy because of physical distancing requirements has resulted in job losses. This is a serious social and economic concern in terms of the type of jobs available in the economy. The adverse response to these job losses has meant a need to find alternative employment. This means there is an urgent need for reskilling and training to suit new employment conditions. From an entrepreneurial policy perspective, governments need to introduce new types of jobs and provide additional training. This can be difficult in the current social climate in which mobility is restricted. In the past, there was an increased emphasis on international mobility but this has been curtailed due to the political changes.

Job changes resulting from the COVID-19 pandemic have been significant. The nature of work has changed with more people working from home. This has resulted in an increase in digital communication for work purposes. The unprecedented move to remote working has caused significant changes in how work is conducted. This has required the use of new digital technologies that can evolve to suit changing workplace needs.

Working from home can save time and money that would otherwise have been incurred in travel costs. This means there are numerous advantages of working from home that need to be evaluated on the basis of the benefits of physical contact. Nonverbal communication in terms of body language provides an important way of understanding messages. This nonverbal communication can be lost in an online format. Thus, new ways of adapting to this change are needed in terms of fostering workplace collaboration. Job demands and control have also changed due to the inability to physically see what tasks are being conducted. Although this can still be seen in a different way by using new technology devices. This has meant that job characteristics are increasingly based on trust and performance. Work hours are now more tailored to an individual's workstyle that is reflected in different ways of working. For some, work might be conducted during normal office hours but for others alternative time periods can be used.

Social policies regarding work/life balance during the COVID-19 pandemic

The COVID-19 pandemic has affected most areas of public and private life. This has resulted in significant lifestyle changes and led to a shift toward digital communication. Since the end of 2019 when the COVID-19 pandemic first stated most regions around the world have been affected with some more than others due to the rate of infection. This has meant an increased reliance on social support to aid those affected. Social support is defined as 'instrumental aid, emotional concern, informational, and appraisal functions of others in the work (family) domain that are intended to enhance the wellbeing of the recipient' (Michel, Kotrba, Mitchelson, Clark and Baltes, 2011:92). Each type of social support works in a different way to alleviate pressures faced by individuals during the COVID-19 pandemic. This social support is important as the COVID-19 pandemic represents a major crisis with the economic, social, and financial effects still ongoing. Some sectors of the global economy notably tourism and hospitality have been affected more than others. This has led to a downturn in tourism and a change in current management practices.

The global economy is expected to contract as a result of the COVID-19 pandemic with the result being worse than previous financial crises. Some sectors including information technology have increased due to the COVID-19 pandemic. The sports industry has been hard hit by the pandemic in terms of financial revenue. Many sport games have had to play behind closed doors with no spectators, which has led to job involvement changes. Job involvement refers to the importance of work to an individual. Increasingly more individuals want a better work/life balance so they focus on job involvement for psychological reasons. The stresses caused by the COVID-19 pandemic have created some forms of work–family conflict due to changing social roles at home. Work–family conflict is defined as 'a form of inter-role conflict in which the role pressures from the work and family domains are mutually incompatible in some respect' (Greenhaus and Beutell, 1985:77). This requires careful consideration by government policy makers in order to increase cohesion in society. To do this, governments can focus on social forms of entrepreneurial policy that help balance work/life issues.

Social entrepreneurship involves creating social value through solving problems faced by society. This involves using different resources to simulate change by developing social goods and services. Social entrepreneurs target unjust systems by transforming them into more sustainable forms of innovation. Context can be understood in terms of where and when (Welter, 2011). The where refers to the geographic location in which the entrepreneurship is conducted. The when refers to the time during which the entrepreneurship took place. Increasingly the temporal aspect of entrepreneurship is becoming more important in terms of the resulting business activity. In certain time periods such as the COVID-19 pandemic more health and digital types of entrepreneurship may emerge in the economy. This will help to create solutions to some of the problems under observation. As businesses face a number of challenges in the COVID-19 environment, it is important to continually reassess goals.

Many people are reconsidering their lifestyles in light of COVID-19. Working from home has become the norm for those who can and this trend is expected to continue in the future. There is an increased emphasis on work/ life balance particularly in terms of physical and mental well-being. Due to

COVID-19 restrictions, individuals have been required to stay at home. This has shaped a new way of living that is reliant on digital technology. As a result of government restrictions, individuals have had to rely more on digital technology for business services. This has created anxiety among some individuals who previously preferred physical contact. This sense of isolation has caused mental health issues that are still yet to be understood. Thus, there needs to be some form of assessment about how to manage risks during the COVID-19 crisis.

Risk management

The word 'risk' tends to have a negative connotation due to the uncertainty it involves. This means it refers to some kind of bad consequence occurring as the result of an action. The severity of these consequences is unknown so it is assumed the effect is negative although it could be positive. Risk can imply a form of loss that might not be able to be recovered. For this reason, there is an ambiguity in the use of the word risk due to the different ways it can be construed. There is a general sense of hazard when referring to risk (Gilligan, 2001). This is due to the high probability of an uncertain outcome. Often individuals and businesses focus too much on risk while neglecting the positive outcomes of doing something different (Masten and Powell, 2003). While the goal from most actions is to receive a positive outcome there can also be learning benefits associated with action. This means the knowledge derived from an action can be more valuable than the resulting outcome. The word risk implies some kind of judgment that is hard to objectively define. This means there is subjectivity on whether something is risky. Individuals who like change may view an action as being normal while others unfamiliar with this occurrence may perceive it as being risky. Therefore, the implicit value associated with risk results in different perceptions. Risk is associated with adversity or hardship as it involves some kind of different behavior. Any kind of decision involves threats and opportunities that need to be carefully managed.

Opportunities and threats need to be assessed in terms of their impact. They do not have to be treated separately, but can be analyzed together in terms of implications. Potential threats can be minimized when appropriate action is taken. This means thinking about possibilities then forming appropriate courses of action. Threats can also be neutralized when examined in the right way. This means there are resulting positive improvements in performance that arise from managing threats in the right way.

Risk can involve uncertain events or circumstances that if it occurs will have different results. The impact of the risk can be high or low depending on the circumstances. With any kind of risk there is potential for advantageous outcomes. This means there is an upside as well as downside to risk. Risks that are perceived as threats tend to be associated with the inadequate flow of information. This results in a poor allocation or use of resources. This can be a deliberate or unintended outcome. As a result, the risk is perceived as an interruption to the normal course of events. Risk means there can be some form of conflict with the intended and unintended outcomes. This means in order to decrease the severity of unintended outcomes, some form of risk management strategy may be introduced. This will reflect an individual's desire to avoid certain risks.

Small businesses have been aware of the need for risk management for a long time, but the COVID-19 pandemic has intensified the need for further planning about mitigating risks. Risk is hard to predict due to the uncertainty about future scenarios. This means that while there can be some estimates of risk it is difficult to estimate correctly the amount of risk. This means data analytics can be used as a probabilistic estimate of risk but miscalculations can still occur. Risk is usually analyzed in terms of probable outcomes which refer to some kind of financial change. This can refer to a decrease in profits, bankruptcy, or other kinds of ruin. Other ways to analyze risk include strategic or competitive rationales. Strategic reasons refer to the expected and actual returns based on some kind of output. This means the actual return on a capital investment might need to be adjusted. Competitive rationales refer to relational risks such as information misinterpretation or incompetent partners.

Small businesses are facing supply chain risks due to uncertainty in the sourcing and delivery of their products. To manage risk, a number of steps should be undertaken. Firstly, identifying what the risk is and then classifying it in terms of urgency. Normally high-impact risks are avoided by small businesses although this is not always possible. In order to avoid risks, some form of avoidance is needed. This means changing the way a business responds to risk by implementing a plan. This will help to protect the small business from potential impact. Uncertainty management is a way to manage risk. This means identifying all different forms of uncertainty without having preconceived ideas. This means all potential sources of uncertainty are examined without implying whether they are desirable or undesirable. This can be due to a lack of certainty around risk.

Small businesses need to reconfigure their organizational design due to the impacts of the COVID-19 pandemic. Organizational design is defined as 'an organization's optimal levels of differentiation and integration given relevant internal and external contingencies' (Foss, 2020:1). The way a small business is designed can be analyzed from a short-term and long-term perspective. In the short term, immediate changes may need to be made related to how the business is conducted. This is reflected in a need to consider occupational health and safety issues in light of COVID-19. Many small changes may need to be made in order to adapt to new market conditions. Not all of these changes will remain in place for the long term as they are reactive strategies. In the long term, major changes may need to be made.

In a business context, the risk is associated with negative variations to expected outcomes. This means risk infers that sometimes certain incidents can occur that lead to an alteration in expected results. This disruption can cause hesitation in business practices due to its unknown nature. To overcome potential disruptions, businesses instigate risk management strategies. This enables ideas to be formulated about expected processes of action. This allows strategies to be implemented that can help decrease the associated impacts from disruption. Some businesses try to diversify their supply chain in order to mitigate potential risk. This can lead to back-up plans being put in place in order to help alleviate shortages. Other risk management techniques include stockpiling or utilizing reserve capacity. This can help in providing more real-time and quality information regarding entrepreneurial opportunities.

Entrepreneurial risk policy during the crisis

The emergence of entrepreneurship as a key policy initiative is logical given the increase in the knowledge and service economy. Entrepreneurs and entrepreneurship are viewed as the key strategic drivers that have shifted the focus of the global economy from the manufacturing sector to one integrating technology and knowledge. As a result, economies have changed from being based on management models to those focusing on entrepreneurship. Public policy now focuses more on promoting policies that support entrepreneurs and facilitates an entrepreneurial culture. While the practical significance of incorporating entrepreneurship into public policy discussions is important, there is lack of knowledge about how entrepreneurial policy is made.

Entrepreneurship is represented in everyday life through actions and situations. While the research field of entrepreneurship is mature, subfields such as entrepreneurial policy are young. This means there is still much uncertainty about what an entrepreneurial policy actually is and how it is manifested in society. The COVID-19 crisis has required governments to respond effectively to the immediate needs of communities. This has meant that COVID-19 has required a massive use of government resources to support the community. To do this, a leadership model emphasizing real-time information and collaboration has been utilized. A successful crisis manager is one who can interact effectively with other government entities in order to deliver a coordinated approach. Managing intergovernmental relationships can be a challenge in a crisis. In order to build collaborative networks, there needs to be frequent interaction and updates about the crisis.

Policy makers try to anticipate crises but this can be hard to do because of their unexpected nature. Crisis management is an important function of government who endeavor to reduce the risk to human life resulting from unexpected events. Managing a crisis is a form of emergency management that involves mitigation, preparedness, response, and recovery (Petak, 1985). Crises can overwhelm a governments' capacity to respond in a timely fashion. This occurs due to a crisis meaning that governments need to obtain resources in order to provide relief to those in need. In times of crises, the government needs to quickly mobilize resources in order to coordinate a joint response. This might include nonhierarchical and non-geographical coordination. To do this can be a complex task as entities from different industries and geographic locations work together.

Increasingly governance networks are being used as a way to encourage collaboration. This enables cooperative relationships to form among previously diverse groups in society. Collaborative interaction is an important way government can respond to crises. By establishing coordinative relationships in a strategic manner, it enables governments to react better. This collaboration relies on mutual interest rather than any formal structure. When a crisis occurs, there is a need for information about how to respond and what resources are required. Coordination lays the groundwork for this response and provides the social underpinnings necessary for successful outcomes. By recognizing the need for concurrent and mutual interaction, network members can better respond to a crisis. This facilitates long-term interactions that provide an effective response. Thereby acknowledging the mutually beneficial trade-offs that derive from collaboration.

Collaboration enables a dynamic set of integrative working relationships to develop that reduces uncertainty. This helps to solve problems and ensure minimal disruption. In a crisis situation, it is important that information is disseminated when needed. This process differs from a normal market environment situation where information is only disseminated to market participants. In order to address response efforts, information needs to be shared that enables interaction to occur. In a highly time-dependent environment information should be exchanged quickly. This will enable community linkages to develop that can facilitate trust. By identifying the patterns of interaction, communities can respond in a more decisive way.

Entrepreneurs are important to the recovery process of any crisis. In rebuilding communities after a crisis or disaster, entrepreneurs can help facilitate the new businesses gaining momentum and encourage a positive community spirit. Entrepreneurs restore disrupted social networks after a recovery that facilitates business development. This means that entrepreneurs proactively engage in constructive behavior that enables a community to open up previously closed services. Chamlee-Wright and Storr (2010) further suggest that entrepreneurs provide a social function in facilitating collective action by providing direct assistance. This helps a community to access resources and advice in times of a crisis. To do this, entrepreneurs act as advocators for social reform. This means that an entrepreneur serves an organizational function in bringing together different entities.

A crisis normally has an uncertain and ongoing timeframe, which is different to a disaster that implies a definable moment. Both crisis and disaster are associated with some form of disruption to daily life. A disaster is defined as 'an event limited in space and time that imposes severe danger, physical damage, and disruption of the routine functioning of society or a part thereof' (Nelson and Lima, 2020:721). This is similar to the concept of entrepreneurship that also involves disruption but normally is associated with a positive event. After a crisis has occurred, there are normally certain associated response mechanisms that take place. This means immediately after a crisis, there is an expected sense of shock and surprise. This can lead to abnormal reactions that might not be properly considered. Due to the sudden nature of a crisis, it can take some time to adjust to the new environment. Depending on the severity of a crisis, the previous environmental conditions may be reactivated quickly but more severe crises might lead to a completely new environment taking shape. The initial confusion resulting from a crisis means there can be competing views about how to proceed. This disorientation makes it difficult to gain confidence in members of the public about the right course of action.

To reestablish a sense of normalcy after a crisis can be a difficult task. It places a heavy demand on those whose job it is to restore confidence in the community. Entrepreneurship is a critical element of the way communities, businesses, and individuals can respond to COVID-19 changes. The introduction of new ways of doing business is central to the idea of entrepreneurship and enables crisis to be turned into opportunities. Undertaking entrepreneurship tends to involve introducing new products or services to the marketplace but can also refer to other activities including a change in mindset. This means entrepreneurship while mostly referring to positive change, can also involve risk-taking activity. Due to the uncertain commercial and technical outcomes resulting from changes in the COVID-19 environment, it is important to assess the level of risk being undertaken by entrepreneurs. A large percentage of entrepreneurial projects tend to fail in their first year so it is essential to understand how societal forces can alter this outcome. The volatility in the market due to COVID-19 changes can both weaken and strengthen market demand depending on the circumstances. This means entrepreneurs may be more willing to make risky investments when the perceived outcome is more positive. The COVID-19 crisis will have a lasting effect on the global economy due to the significant digital disruption it has caused. The incentives for entrepreneurship have changed due to the need for digital considerations in business models. This has resulted in a process of creative destruction in which there has been a reallocation toward digital businesses.

Conclusion

This chapter has focused on the risks derived from the COVID-19 crisis. These risks impact small businesses in a profound way and will influence future courses of action. As discussed in the chapter, small businesses have had to use entrepreneurship in order to find new opportunities. This means emphasizing the possibilities of introducing different product or service categories into the marketplace. To do this, small businesses need to carefully evaluate their risks and likelihood of success.

References

Adger, W. (2000) 'Social and ecological resilience: Are they related?', *Progress in Human Geography*, 24(3): 347–364.

Alvarez, S. A. and Barney, J. B. (2007) 'Discovery and creation: Alternative theories of entrepreneurial action', *Strategic Entrepreneurship Journal*, 1(1–2): 11–26.

Amoros, J. (2020) 'Guest editorial: Management research and Covid-19: A quick response for action in Iberoamerica', *Management Research: Journal of the Iberoamerican Academy of Management*, 18(4): 345–356.

Bapuji, H., Patel, C., Ertug, G. and Allen, D. (2020) 'Corona crisis and inequality: Why management research needs a societal turn', *Journal of Management*, 46(7): 1205–1222.

Baum, J. R. and Locke, E. A. (2004) 'The relationship of entrepreneurial traits, skill, and motivation to subsequent venture growth', *Journal of Applied Psychology*, 89(4): 587.

Cardon, M. S., Wincent, J., Singh, J. and Drnovsek, M. (2009) 'The nature and experience of entrepreneurial passion', *Academy of Management Review*, 34(3): 511–532.

Chamlee-Wright, E. and Storr, V. H. (2010) 'Expectations of government's response to disaster', *Public Choice*, 144(1–2): 253–274.

Chen, X. P., Yao, X. and Kotha, S. (2009) 'Entrepreneur passion and preparedness in business plan presentations: A persuasion analysis of venture capitalists' funding decisions', *Academy of Management Journal*, 52(1): 199–214.

Edoho, F. M. (2015) 'Entrepreneurship and socioeconomic development: Catalyzing African transformation in the 21st century', *African Journal of Economic and Management Studies*, 6(2): 127–147.

Foss, N. (2020) 'The impact of the Covid-19 pandemic on firm's organisational designs', *Journal of Management Studies*, In Press.

Gilligan, R. (2001) *Promoting resilience: A resource guide on working with children in the care system.* London: British Agencies for Adoption and Fostering.

Gonzalez, M., Husted, B. and Aigner, D. (2017) 'Opportunity discovery and creation in social entrepreneurship: An exploratory study in Mexico', *Journal of Business Research*, 81: 212–220.

Greenhaus, J. H. and Beutell, N. J. (1985) 'Sources of conflict between work and family roles', *Academy of Management Review*, 10(1): 76–88.

Hisrich, R. D. and Peters, M. P. (2002) *Entrepreneurship*, 5th ed. Sydney: McGraw-Hill/ Irwin.

Johannesson, G. T. (2012) 'To get things done: A relational approach to entrepreneurship', *Scandinavian Journal of Hospitality and Tourism*, 12(2): 181–196.

Lewis, V. L. and Churchill, N. C. (1983) 'The five stages of small business growth', *Harvard Business Review*, 61(3): 30–50.

Masten, A. S. and Powell, J. L. (2003) 'A resilience framework for research, policy, and practice', In S. S. Luthar (Ed.), *Resilience and vulnerability: Adaptation in the context of childhood adversities* (pp. 1–28). New York: Cambridge University Press.

Michel, J. S., Kotrba, L. M., Mitchelson, J. K., Clark, M. A. and Baltes, B. B. (2011) 'Antecedents of work–Family conflict: A meta-analytic review', *Journal of Organizational Behavior*, 32(5): 689–725.

Nelson, R. and Lima, E. (2020) 'Effectuations, social bricolage and causation in the response to a natural disaster', *Small Business Economics*, 54: 721–750.

Petak, W. (1985) 'Emergency management: A challenge for public administration', *Public Administration Review*, 45: 3–7.

Ratten, V. (2016) 'Sport innovation management: Towards a research agenda', *Innovation Management, Policy & Practice*, 18(3): 238–250.

Ratten, V. and Dana, L.-P. (2017) 'Sustainable entrepreneurship, family farms and the dairy industry', *International Journal of Social Ecology and Sustainable Development*, 8(3): 114–129.

Ratten, V., Ferreira, J. J. and Fernandes, C. I. (2017) 'Innovation management – Current trends and future directions', *International Journal of Innovation and Learning*, 22(2): 135–155.

Sarasvathy, S. D., Dew, N., Velamuri, S. R. and Venkataraman, S. (2003) 'Three views of entrepreneurial opportunity', In *Handbook of entrepreneurship research* (pp. 141–160). Boston, MA: Springer.

Venkatesh, V. (2020) 'Impacts of Covid-19: A research agenda to support people in their fight', *International Journal of Information Management*, In Press.

Walker, B., Holling, C., Carpenter, S. and Kinzig, A. (2004) 'Resilience, adaptability, and transformability in social-ecological systems', *Ecology and Society*, 9(2): 5.

Welter, F. (2011) 'Contextualizing entrepreneurship – Conceptual challenges and ways forward', *Entrepreneurship theory and Practice*, 35(1): 165–184.

4 Impact of COVID-19 on MSMEs in India

The Black Swan event that might change the trajectory of India's economic growth

Sandeep Bhasin and Bhawna Kumar

Introduction

It is incredible that Micro Small and Medium Enterprises (MSME) sector alone contributes to almost 45% of the total employment opportunities in India, 50% of total exports from India, 29% of total country's gross domestic product (GDP), and 95% of total industrial units in the country. The Central Government plans a contribution of $2 trillion from the MSMEs, which will eventually lead India in accomplishing the goal to become a $5 trillion economy by 2024 (Ministry of MSME, 2020). All this was till the virus ruptured the economy, and with it, the MSME sector. Figure 4.1 depicts the distribution of MSME in India.

In an interview given to one of the leading business newspapers of India, a senior representative of the Ministry of Micro, Small, and Medium Enterprises

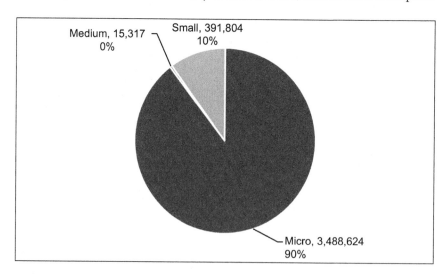

Figure 4.1 Distribution of MSME in India

Source: Author's own

indicated that over a 100 million jobs could be lost because of the slump in the economy. MSMEs depend on the trade with three major trading partners the United States, China, and Europe (Kumar, 2020), and with any disruption on these would directly impact the performance of MSMEs. With the spread of the virus across the globe, coupled with lockdowns imposed by the State and Central Governments in the country, MSMEs started feeling the pressure. The reasons for this sudden slump included nonavailability of migrant laborers (who worked as temporary laborers in MSMEs), sudden drop in the demand of goods, and nonavailability of funds for the MSMEs (Ministry of MSME, 2020; Nishtha, 2020). In this chapter, we will look at the impact of spread of COVID-19 on Indian MSME sector in short to midterm with a focus on select industries and the steps the government has taken to ensure minimizing the impact of this Black Swan Event. To understand the impact on Entrepreneurship development in India, we have liberally used the GEM Model as proposed by William D. Bygrave and Andrew Zacharakis.

The society and the culture

The contribution of entrepreneurs to the U.S. GDP stands at 44%. Comparing this, Indian entrepreneurs contribute less than 2% of India's GDP. The difference lies in the definition and categorization of the term Entrepreneur. While the U.S. Government has gone to the extreme to help the entrepreneurs register patents and establish businesses (US Small Business Administration Office of Advocacy, 2020), the government in the third-world countries, especially India did not pay attention to the entrepreneurs but concentrated on helping small and medium manufacturers, traders, and service providers. When this segment included while calculating, the contribution of MSMEs to India's GDP is over 29%. These manufacturers, traders, and service providers may not fit into the new definition of entrepreneurs who follow at least one of the four innovations, viz., *Product innovation, Organization innovation, Process innovations,* and/or *Market Innovation.* A case in point is the number of patents filed in India in the past 13 years. According to a report published by the Department of Science and Technology, Government of India, 76% of the patents filed in India in the last 13 years were filed by foreign-based entities (Kumar C, 2020) including Qualcomm and Huawei. Even as the government encourages the stakeholders to get innovative and file for patents, what stops Indians is the low level of research and development. On an average, India spent under 0.7% of its GDP (adjusted to PPP) on research and development (Das, 2019) as compared to China's 10% (Normile, 2020) and the United States' 27% (Congressional Research Service, 2020). With such low budgets spent on R&D, the Indian corporates find it difficult to compete in global markets. So, where are the Indians going wrong?

Indians have traditionally been a risk-averse society and this is evident in the manner in which the kids are brought up in families. Almost all of the education of the kids is taken care by the parents (HSBC Survey, 2017). Over 90% of marriages (Rukmini, 2018) are arranged marriages where the youngsters are not allowed to take the decision of choosing their life partners. It is always discouraged to let the kids ask questions to the elders in the family as a tradition and this is another reason of why the Indian youth feel restricted in independent thinking. The culture of the country is one of the major determinants for it to become an entrepreneurial economy and this is evident when we consider the United States, where youngsters are encouraged to live an independent life even as they approach puberty. With the young taking their life's decisions, they inculcate the risk-taking capability as part of their personality. These cultural values play not only an important but also a defining role to which a society considers entrepreneurial behavior and decision-making. Many studies, especially by researchers including Herbig and Hofstede, have proved under the set parameters that cultures which reward risk-taking and independent thinking behavior promote one of the four basic innovations (Product Innovation, Market Innovation, Organizational Innovation, and Process Innovation), whereas cultures which are overprotective toward the young, restrict growth of entrepreneurial spirit within the community. The role of the family, immediate and extended, is recognized as having the potential to make a positive contribution toward entrepreneurial behavior through the provision of intergenerational role models, and as tangible and intangible support providers (Morrison, 2000).

Among other societal factors, corruption in the society plays an important role in development of entrepreneurial spirit. High levels of corruption have a negative effect on entrepreneurship (Liu, Hu, Zhang and Carrick, 2019). Corruption is an inseparable part of the culture of any society. Our belief is that the economic corruption affects entrepreneurial activity as it directly impacts the trust factor in the society and as a result increases the costs of doing business. Logically, the stakeholders involved in ventures have to not only budge for bribes to be paid to the officials but also monitor other stakeholders' activities on a constant basis as the trust factor is generally the lowest in such societies.

The politics and policies

The policies followed by the governments across the markets (whether emerging or developed) define the trajectory of the growth, especially in the standard of living of the stakeholders. For a country such as India, the policies were centralized toward Small and Medium Enterprises (SMEs) and then toward MSMEs. The concept of entrepreneurs was not recognized by any of the democratically elected governments. Defining the role of entrepreneurs or that of MSMEs in the growth of an economy may turn out to be a bit controversial as we strongly believe that the nation must concentrate on the Ends rather than the *Means*. In India's case, the contribution of MSMEs to the national growth (measured by the GDP) stands at 29% of GDP. The Ministry of MSME has already set a target of 50% of contribution toward the GDP coming from MSME by 2024. Considering the flow of activities as presented in Figure 4.1, the growth of SMEs would directly depend on the growth of large corporates.

Table 4.1 New definition of MSMEs

MSME classification (₹ 1 crore = US $ 136,000 (Appx.)			
Criteria	Micro	Small	Medium
Investment	<₹1 crore	<₹10 crores	<₹50 crores
and	and	and	and
Annual turnover	<₹5 crores	<₹50 crores	<₹250 crores

Source: Author's own

To understand this relationship, we must understand the policies of the government especially created to support small manufacturers and service providers. To do this, it is important to state the MSME classification in terms of micro-, small-, and medium-sized criteria in terms of investment and annual turnover. This is stated in Table 4.1.

Some of the initiatives taken by the Government of India during pandemic are:

1   An emergency credit line of ₹300,000 crores for MSMEs from Banks and Non-Banking Financial Institutions (NBFCs). The tenure for this would be 4 years with moratorium of 12 months on principal payment.
2   Stressed MSMEs will get ₹20,000 crores (US$ 2.70 billion) of subordinate debt. Under the scheme, the promoters will be given debt by banks, which will get infused as Promoter's equity into the MSME.
3   MSMEs will be able to avail benefits of additional equity infusion of up to ₹50,000 crores (US$ 6.8 billion) via Fund of Funds.
4   The Indian Government to disallow Global Tenders of up to ₹200 crores (US$ 27 million) from foreign companies, thus giving a fillip to local players, especially MSMEs.
5   The government will take initiative to develop an e-marketplace for MSMEs to bridge the gap between the corporates and MSMEs.

Apart from these, the Government of India is working on creating an incubator for MSMEs, under which close to 70% of the cost of innovation will be absorbed by the Government. Similarly, the government has taken the initiative to promote women entrepreneurs by offering them funds, mentoring program, and financing.

1   Priority sector lending: Direct and indirect finance at subsidized interest rates will include all MSMEs.
2   Credit Guarantee Fund Scheme: Collateral free credit to micro and small enterprises.
3   Purchase Preference Policy: Group of items are reserved exclusively for purchase from MSMEs.

4   Price Preference Policy: For select goods that are manufactured by both small-scale and large-scale enterprises, a price preference of 15% is offered to small-scale manufacturers over the lowest bid received.
5   Benefits in tendering: MSMEs can avail benefits such as exemption on payment of earnest money deposits, exemption on payment of security deposits, etc.
6   Raw Material assisted scheme by National Small Industries Corporation (NSIC): NSIC finances the purchase of raw material.

The schemes introduced by the government are a good beginning. However, the performance of MSMEs completely depends on the performance of the large corporates, as almost all the MSMEs directly or indirectly depend on supplying the material to the large corporates. A report published by Brick-work Rating, close to ₹3.3 lakh crores (US$ 41 billion) worth of MSME funds were stuck with strong large corporates in the form of receivables in June 2020 (Brickworks, 2020). The figures are quite big given the size of MSMEs in the country, which takes us back to the basis of GEM Model of study. In Figure 4.1, this aspect is represented with the linkage of SMEs with the large corporates as both are interdependent on each other, with large corporates having an advantage of bargaining power over SMEs. With the new initiatives launched by the government of India, it is this dependence that gets funded by the new schemes; even as more than 35% of MSMEs and small businesses started closing down unable to take the pressure of the spread of virus (Saluja, 2020). However, the government has refuted this news. As of July 2020, the banks had already sanctioned ₹1.37 lakh crores to MSMEs. This comes after the government included large firms, doctors, and lawyers into the MSME loan guarantee scheme (Nair, 2020).

The general national framework conditions

Role of the government: what, where, when, why, and how of lockdown

The lockdown came as a surprise to the country on March 24, 2020, when the Prime Minister of the Country Mr. Modi came on National Television to announce the same for the next 21 days. This was just the beginning of the long process of lockdowns that lasted till May 31, 2020. India went into lockdown when there were less than 1000 infection cases registered. When India started the process of Unlock, or opening up of the nation, India had over 10,000 daily cases reported. There has been no drop since and India has crossed over 100,000 COVID-related deaths.

During the lockdown, the government restricted the movement of citizens out of home, and this directly impacted the commercial interest of the country. According to one estimate, India lost over ₹30 lakh crores (Approximately USD 410 billion) during the lockdown (Shukla, 2020). The relief package announced by the government was approximately 50% of this amount, which

Table 4.2 Lockdown and unlock 2020

Phase	Dates
Lockdown	
Phase 1	March 25–April 14, 2020
Phase 2	April 15–May 3, 2020
Phase 3	May 4–May 17, 2020
Phase 4	May 18–May 31, 2020
Unlock	
Unlock 1.0	June 1–June 30, 2020
Unlock 2.0	July 1–July 31, 2020
Unlock 3.0	August 1–August 31, 2020
Unlock 4.0	September 1–September 30, 2020
Unlock 5.0	October 1–October 31, 2020

Source: Author's own

raised many questions. Couple that with the late addition of lawyers, doctors, and large firms in the gambit of revised definition, the process was looked at with some skepticism. Table 4.2 states the phases and dates of each lockdown period.

With the economy spiraling down, the government had limited choice but to allow the State Governments to open up the place of work, especially the manufacturing sector. This was the beginning of Unlock 1.0 on June 1, 2020. But by this time, India had not peaked its COVID-19-related infection, and the COVID-19-related deaths continued at a high pace. This has raised new questions on whether it was required to lockdown the economy in the first place (Bhattacharyya, 2020). While the jury is still out there on whether the lockdown was the right strategy to implement at the given moment, the impact on the MSMEs was quite severe. As the lockdown started, majority of the workforce, the migrant laborers, moved back to their homes (Migrant Exodus, 2020). According to an estimate, over ten million laborers were displaced because of the lockdown (Sharma, 2020). This exodus impacted the MSMEs' working to a great extent. With low labor availability, it directly impacted the costs, resulting in more losses for the MSMEs.

Even as the economy crawls back to normalcy, it is estimated that the recovery process would take additional 8 months (Singh, 2020). Moody's, one of the world's leading ratings agency, expected India's economy to contract 11.5% in the fiscal year ending March 2021 (Moody's Investor Service, 2020; Rebello, 2020).

The 'stagnant' growth of MSMEs

While across the globe, the medium grows into big, in India, most of the businesses start small, stay small, and die small, which is a concern for the policy makers. This is the result of failing to scale with growth in the market space.

One of the factors that directly contribute to this failure is the level of innovation in this sector. Even as the government promotes innovation, the state of patents filed over a period of time has been a major concern. Majority of patents filed come from MNCs and foreign nationals in India.

Looking outward, the dominance of large players and their negotiation power forces SMEs to stay small. Even as we don't have dependable data from India related to the productivity of SMEs (Bhattacharya, 2020), the data from MSMEs operating in the manufacturing sector in OECD countries show that the productivity of medium enterprises (between 50 and 250 employees) could be near 80% higher than that of microenterprises (with less than 9 employees). The relative growth in scale at which they operate allows them to invest in people (improved skill sets), in the latest technology, and updated processes, leading to innovation at work.

The dynamics of a country's industrial structure changes with the growth and improvement of capabilities and productivity of MSMEs. Productivity of MSMEs can define its growth over a period of time. When we compare the structure of SMEs in India and Bangladesh in the textile sector, we observe that one of the largest textile cluster of India, Tirupur, has 70% units with less than ten employees as compared to just 20% of units (with less than ten employees) in Narayanganj in Bangladesh. The smaller size of the enterprises directly impacts the productivity of these enterprises and thus creating an impact on the competitive advantage of these enterprises in a highly competitive market. The government's failure in supporting the growth of these microenterprises over the years has impacted the competitive advantage in the industry. A similar decline in competitive advantage India enjoyed in Cotton production and processing can be observed even as China manages to create its space in the marketplace.

The availability of finance

With nearly 90% of MSMEs in the micro category with less than ten employees (refer Chart 1), the challenge for the government is to ensure the availability of finance to help these microenterprises sail through such unpredictability. The pressure on MSMEs has been increasing with the increase in global competition. Couple this with the pressure after the spread of the COVID-19 pandemic, we observe a spike in bad loans related to MSMEs (Mahajan, Sinha and Prabhavati, 2020).

With the spike in bad loans given to MSMEs over the last years, the future funds availability to run the enterprises declines as the allocation of funds is done depending on the credit score, the enterprise, and the promoters. This vicious circle creates a serious impact on the performance of the Banks and NBFCs (Axis Capital).

Even as the MSME sector contributes 29% toward the GDP of India, on an average the loans as a percentage of total loan book for leading banks is in the region of 12%. This discrepancy elevates the fact that banks in general have been a little stringent in making the credit available to MSMEs. This is quite evident when we do a Year-on-Year comparison between the loan book of banks operating in India. The total loan book of banks in India declined to ₹67 lakh crores (approximately $915 billion) in June from nearly Rs. 70 lakh crores (approximately $956 billion) a year ago in June 2019 (Mahajan et al., 2020). Of this figure, only ₹16.9 lakh crores (approximately $230.7 billion) were lent to MSMEs. Government of India launched Emergency Credit Line Guarantee Scheme (ECLGS) to help the MSMEs with much-needed funds during the spread of COVID-19. However, in spite of the Government-backed credit scheme, only 2.6 times higher loans were disbursed to the sector between February and June 2020. It may be noted that the lockdown started on March 24 and ended on May 31, 2020. The reason for such a dismal performance of the scheme was the fact that only 50% of the MSMEs were eligible for the credit line under the ECLGS scheme (Shukla, 2020). One of the reasons for this low rate of acceptance of the scheme is low overall demand of the product/service produced by the MSMEs. Many MSMEs preferred to observe the demand pattern of their products to decide on applying for the ECLGS scheme. Overall, there was a dip of funding by 50% during the nationwide lockdown, as compared to the pre-COVID-19 level, with over 50% startups failing to raise additional funding (Saloni, 2020). Close to 15% of the startups were forced to discontinue operations (FICCI/IAN Survey, 2020).

The future of MSMEs

The size of the MSMEs does matter in long-term survival of the enterprise. With close to 90% of MSMEs fall in the microenterprise category, the challenge for the government is not just to help the enterprises survive such Black Swan crises but also build a sustainable future.

Access to loans: Any negative impact on the demand would lead to disruption. For Black Swan events such as spread of COVID-19 virus, we witnessed a huge drop in the demand directly impacting the MSMEs. This drop in demand, coupled with the nonpayment of dues by the large corporates, has created a vacuum of funds. Making the loans available to the MSMEs at reduced rate of interest and ensuring minimal paperwork would help the MSMEs regain their lost grounds.

Engaging with the Government: With the Government targeting 50% of GDP contribution from the MSMEs by 2024, an engagement with the government in policy decisions will add a fillip to the projected growth. The Government can work closely with the MSMEs and designated MSME associations to carve policies that would not only help the MSMEs survive but also build a sustainable future.

Availability of technology: With fairly limited money spent on research and development by the MSMEs, the future role of the enterprises appears limited. MSMEs must allocate funds for R&D-related activities and work with Government-sponsored innovation hubs to ensure better control over commercial patents.

Discover newer markets: With the help from the government and active participation from the specialized industry bodies, MSMEs must work toward creating a global market for their products, rather than restricting to local or regional markets. This may help the MSMEs to lower the dependency of local markets, thus addressing the issue of cyclicity of the business.

References

Annual Report, Ministry of MSME (2020), https://msme.gov.in/sites/default/files/FINAL_MSME_HINDI_AR_2019-20.pdf, last visited 13th November 2020.

Axis Capital (2020), www.axiscapital.co.in, last visited 13th November 2020.

Brickworks Rating, www.brickworkratings.com/Research/BWR_MSME%20note.pdf, last visited 13th November 2020.

Bhattacharya, A. (2020) 'OECD database/The missing LARGE in MSMEs', *Financial Express*, 24th August 2020, www.financialexpress.com/opinion/the-missing-large-in-msmes-a-globally-competitive-indian-mittelstand-is-the-need-of-the-hour/2063155/, last visited 13th November 2020.

Bhattacharyya, I. (2020) 'Why India's lockdown has been a spectacular failure', *The Wire*, 12th June 2020, https://thewire.in/government/india-covid-19-lockdown-failure, last visited 13th November 2020.

Bygrave, W. D. and Zacharakis, A. (2014) *Entrepreneurship*. New York: John Wiley & Sons, ISBN-10.

Congressional Research Service (2020), https://crsreports.congress.gov, last visited 13th November 2020.

FICCI/IAN Survey (2020), http://ficci.in/spdocument/23280/FICCI-IAN-Survey-Covid-19-Start-ups.pdf, last visited 13th November 2020.

HSBC Survey – India (2017), www.about.hsbc.co.in%2F-%2Fmedia%2Findia%2Fen%2Fnews-and-media%2F170702-press-release-value-of-education.pdf&usg=AOvVaw0lHot6tO3T6sskBICp5Cvh, last visited 13th November 2020.

Kumar, A. (2020), https://economictimes.indiatimes.com/jobs/uncertain-future-over-100-million-jobs-in-danger-across-the-country-due-to-covid-19/articleshow/77232289.cms, last visited 13th November 2020.

Kumar, C. (2020) *The Times of India, September 10, 2020; Science and technology indicators*, Department of Science and Technology, Government of India, https://timesofindia.indiatimes.com/india/Ordnance-unions-write-to-defence-minister/articleshow/78035286.cms, last visited 13th November 2020.

Liu, J., Hu, M., Zhang, H. and Carrick, J. (2019) 'Corruption and entrepreneurship in emerging markets', *Emerging Markets Finance and Trade*, 55(5): 1051–1068.

Mahajan, V., Sinha, S. and Prabhavati, R. (2020), www.transunioncibil.com/resources/tucibil/doc/insights/reports/report-msme-pulse-january-2020.pdf, last visited 13th November 2020.

Migrant Exodus (2020), www.financialexpress.com/industry/sme/migrants-exodus-labour-shortage-looms-manufacturing-units-msmes-may-be-worst-hit-says-india-ratings/2049908/, last visited 13th November 2020.

Ministry of Micro, Small and Medium Enterprises, Government of India, https://msme.gov.in

Morrison, A. (2000) 'Entrepreneurship: What triggers it?', *International Journal of Entrepreneurial Behaviour & Research*, 6(2): 59–71.

Nair, R. (2020) *The print*, 1st August 2020, https://theprint.in/economy/govt-expands-msme-loan-guarantee-scheme-to-include-lawyers-doctors-large-firms/472571/, last visited 13th November 2020.

Nishtha, S. (2020) *The Economic Times/All India manufacturers organization*, 2nd June 2020, https://economictimes.indiatimes.com/small-biz/sme-sector/over-one-third-msmes-start-shutting-shop-as-recovery-amid-covid-19-looks-unlikely-aimo-survey/articleshow/76141969.cms, last visited 13th November 2020.

Normile, N. (2020) *Science magazine; OECD data*, 28th August 2020, www.sciencemag.org/news/2020/08/china-again-boosts-rd-spending-more-10, last visited 13th November 2020.

Rebello J. (2020) *The Economic Times/Covid disruption will hurt MSME recovery prospect*, 12th September 2020/Moodys Investors Service, https://economictimes.indiatimes.com/small-biz/sme-sector/covid-disruption-will-hurt-msme-recovery-prospects-says-moodys/articleshow/78164281.cms?from=mdr.

Rukmini (2018) *The Mint*, 4th October 2018, www.livemint.com/Politics/mnVzCflEbqvzEu01LTxqLM/Urban-Indians-still-get-married-the-way-their-grandparents-d.html, last visited 13th November 2020.

Saloni, S. (2020) 'One half of eligible MSMEs able to tap credit line', *The Economic Times*, September 24, 2020. https://economictimes.indiatimes.com/small-biz/sme-sector/only-half-of-eligible-msmes-able-to-tap-the-emergency-credit-line/articleshow/78287193.cms, last visited 13th November 2020.

Sharma, N. (2020) *Quartz India*, 14th September 2020, https://qz.com/india/1903018/indias-covid-19-lockdown-displaced-at-least-10-million-migrants/, last visited 13th November 2020.

Shukla, A. (2020), www.newindianexpress.com/business/2020/may/26/covid-19-caused-economic-loss-of-rs-303-lakh-crore-maharashtra-tamil-nadu-worst-hit-report-2148164.html, last visited 13th November 2020.

Singh, A. (2020), www.dnb.co.in/EDM/FILE/2020/AUG/11/DNB-Webinar-Next-Normal-for-MSMEs.pdf, last visited 13th November 2020.

US Small Business Administration Office of Advocacy, https://advocacy.sba.gov/2020/09/10/small-business-lending-in-the-united-states-2019/, last visited 13th November 2020.

5 Digital transformation from COVID-19 in small business and sport entities

Vanessa Ratten and Ashleigh-Jane Thompson

Introduction

In order for small businesses to get ahead of the changes necessitated by COVID-19, they need to reconfigure their value proposition (Venkatesh, 2020). To do this, they need to focus on the process of digital transformation through the use of information communications and technology. Information and customer engagement needs to be reshaped as a result of the COVID-19 pandemic (Kang, Diao and Zanini, 2020). This means recognizing what is being affected and how it can be delivered through digital technology. To do this means considering in greater detail how customer requirements have changed due to physical and social distancing requirements (Anggadwita, Ramadani, Alamanda, Ratten and Hashani, 2016). This may mean a greater usage of digital technology in the supply chain. Hinings, Gegenhuber and Greenwood (2018:52) define the word digital as being 'the conversion from mainly analog information into the binary language understood by computers.' Digital technology makes it easier to transfer and store knowledge in an online format. Digitalization is an evolutionary process that creates digital competences in order to obtain value. This enhances the customer experience and is fundamental in the creation of new digital services (Ferreira, Fernandes, Peris-Ortiz and Ratten, 2017). Netflix is a good example of a company that has followed the digitalization path. Originally the company rented movies that were sent via the postal services. This changed on an online streaming service that utilized digital technologies. Data are now gathered from customer's online viewing habits to suggest additional services.

In this chapter, a new perspective of entrepreneurship embracing the digital changes resulting from the COVID-19 pandemic is explained. The chapter highlights the importance of entrepreneurship in times of crisis and the dynamic interrelationship between entrepreneurs and society. By adopting an entrepreneurship perspective, it is argued that the legitimacy of entrepreneurs drives change in times of crisis. With COVID-19 entrepreneurship research in its infancy, this chapter offers new conceptual insights into the process of digital transformation.

The aim of this chapter is threefold. First, the impact of COVID-19 on small businesses is discussed in terms of digital transformation. This provides an understanding of how small businesses have moved to a digital format. Second, how small businesses have increased their digital capabilities is discussed in terms of the entrepreneurship and management literature. Third, analysis and synthesis of existing COVID-19 entrepreneurship research are undertaken in terms of understanding the linkages with digital technology. This will enable future research directions and practical implications regarding digital transformation in small business to be highlighted. As such, it can be argued that this chapter provides a wealth of information for connecting COVID-19 to small business research in light of digital technology innovations. This will enable a better understanding of how small business can advance their digital capabilities. To do this, the purpose of this chapter is to shed light on digital transformation in times of crisis. To this end, the chapter aims to address the following research questions:

> RQ1: What are the key motivators behind small business entrepreneur's decision to utilize digital technology in the COVID-19 crisis?
> RQ2: What kind of mechanisms (both financial and social) exists to help small business entrepreneurs utilize digital technology in the COVID-19 crisis?

Digital transformation

Digital transformation involves profound changes that occur based on new digital technologies. Vial (2019:118) defines digital transformation as 'a process that aims to improve an entity by triggering significant changes to its properties through combinations of information, computing, communication and connectivity technologies.' Thus, digital transformation means changing a firm's offerings into a digital format. This can augment or replace physical offerings to make them more easily transferrable. The fourth industrial revolution is characterized by the internet of things in which technology devices are interconnected (Dalmarco, Ramalho, Barros and Soares, 2019). This has emphasized the need to fuse technology with virtual processes to increase usability. The first industrial revolution concerned the mechanization of devices, which meant a change in agricultural production from handmade to include the use of mechanical operations. This spurred economic growth and fueled a growth in cities. The second industrial revolution concerned the electrification of society. This brought increased abilities for factories to continue operating throughout the day. In addition, it enabled increased work efficiency by enabling people to work longer hours. The third industrial revolution involved computerization. This incorporated the use of computers for a range of tasks that were previously performed by humans. The efficiencies from computerization improved knowledge flows and resulted in performance gains. The fourth industrial revolution went further by incorporating the use of artificial intelligence into computing processes. Dalmarco et al. (2019:2) describe the fourth industrial revolution as involving 'the creation of devices capable of acquiring experience over time, communicating with one another and making decisions, leading them to self-optimization.' This means that the fourth industrial revolution is characterized by flexible internet-based production systems that speed up the delivery of services.

In order to facilitate digital transformation, organizational leaders need to develop a digital mindset. This enables the organization to respond to change based on the use of digital technologies. Digital transformation can be described as 'the combined effects of several digital innovations bringing about novel actors (and constellations), structures, practices, values and beliefs that change, threaten, replace or complement existing rules of the game within organisations, ecosystems, industries or field' (Hinings et al., 2018:53). This means that digital transformation requires the integral use of information technology in most areas of an organization through the use of innovation. Therefore, every aspect of an organization will utilize information technology in an innovative way. It can be hard for organizations to move to a digital business model when there are deeply embedded relationships existing with customers and suppliers that utilize existing business models (Santos, Marques, Ferreira, Gerry and Ratten, 2017). Thus, it can take time to change as well-established stakeholders also need to embrace a process of digitalization.

Digital technologies can result in value creation due to efficiency and performance gains (Ratten, 2014). This means the use of digital technology can radically improve the reach of enterprises in terms of adding new customers or markets (Ferreira, Ratten and Dana, 2017). This results in major business improvements based on the creation of new business models. Information technology is the means used to digitalize products and services. Digital technology, including big data, cloud computing, and social media, leads to an increase in digitalization. The health and well-being of society are of central importance. The pace of technology change in some organizations has been slow due to a reluctance to use digital technologies. Digital technology involves the use of analytics, embedded devices, and mobile access to enable more efficient business services. This includes real-time access to services based on the idea of user-generated content. This means there is an emphasis on continual improvement both in the technology utilized to provide the service but also through the way consumers interact with the service. This leads to increased efficiencies in customer service and better streamlining of existing services. Digital transformation then results from focusing holistically on the benefits of technology innovation rather than just a functional mindset of how they can be operationalized in the marketplace.

Digital technology enables small businesses to customize their marketing to certain sociodemographic groups. This enables them to build better relationships and improves overall efficiencies. There has been a rapid growth in the use of digital technologies, which has resulted in increased levels of data being collected each day. This data if used in the right way can provide strategic intelligence that can help organizations obtain a market advantage. Despite the popularity of digital technology, many organizations fail to utilize data in the right way. This is due to there being a disconnection between data obtained and its usefulness for strategy implementation. The business models of small businesses have been rapidly transformed through the pervasiveness of high-speed internet services. This has enabled small businesses to utilize digital technology in their activities and processes for value creation. The advantage of digital transformation is evident in the way small businesses create related products and services. Digital technology enables ideas and information to be linked in an online format. This enables new opportunities to emerge that are more consistent with customer needs.

Contemporary small businesses need to change their business operations in order to take advantage of digital innovations. Small businesses have been able to utilize mobile computing in order to widen their consumer market. This means instead of relying on physical buildings, they can be more mobile in moving to find new customer segments. This flexibility has enabled small businesses to compete with others in a way that was not previously possible. In order to take advantage of digital technology, small businesses need to focus on strategy instead of the technology. This digital consciousness enables small businesses to develop competences that can be leveraged through technology.

In the digital marketplace, consumers are using mobile communication devices to make purchasing decisions. This involves utilizing real-time data provided in an interactive format based on user specifications. As a result, consumers are deciding who to purchase from based on data available on the internet. Due to the increased amount of data available online, consumers are also reading online reviews to decide what to buy (Ratten, 2015). This has shifted businesses marketing strategies to a more online format in order to rethink their current capabilities. There has been an explosion of online data that if utilized in the right way can provide strategic advantages for a business. For small businesses, the digital transformation raises a number of issues that can be analyzed in terms of context and characteristics. This is summarized in Table 5.1.

Table 5.1 Systemization of issues related to digital transformation

Field of inquiry	*Issues to be raised*
Context	What are the similarities and differences for small business between the pre-COVID-19 environment regarding digital technology and the current COVID-19 environment?
	What environmental factors explain the usage of digital technology for COVID-19 entrepreneurship purposes?
	What importance is placed on digital technology to survive during the COVID-19 crisis?
	How have small businesses adopted digital technology during the COVID-19 crisis?
Characteristics	How do small businesses compared to large businesses differ in their usage of digital technology?
	What kinds of digital technology have become important because of the COVID-19 crisis?
	In what way does digital technology help small businesses?

Source: Author developed

Crisis and digital technology

It is important to manage a business in times of crisis to ensure its continuity. This process is called business continuity management and enables businesses to survive in times of hardship. Gomez, Mendoza, Ramirez and Olivas-Lujan (2020:404) refer to business continuity management as 'the set of processes focused on reducing organizational impact and protect the key stakeholders (e.g. communities and employees) of an eventuality.' The main stages involved in business continuity management are mitigation, preparation, response, and recovery (SchWeber, 2013). Each of these stages reflects different courses of action a business should follow. In the mitigation stage, it is useful to have alternative courses of action available to the business. This means when a crisis occurs, the business manager is ready to change paths. The preparation stage means having the resources and information available to make the best decisions. To do this means obtaining the right advice but also implementing specific actions. The response stage refers to actions actually taken in times of crisis. Businesses respond in different ways so it is important to consider the implications of certain actions. The recovery stage involves trying to bounce back from a time of inertia. This might mean hiring new people or building upon existing resources.

All small businesses play a key role in minimizing the effect of COVID-19 on society. Social crises such as poverty and hunger tend to occur more in developing countries. Other types of crises such as climate change have a worldwide effect but tend to occur over a longer time period. Governments around the world have closed borders and canceled social activities to decrease the spread of the virus. While this strategy has been successful, it has also led to psychological distress and mental health issues. The government interventions have been put in place to lower the number of infections but have economic ramifications. Currently, small business managers are navigating troubled waters that require specific action. This has resulted in overwhelming challenges for small business managers that have costly effects.

The management of a crisis has financial and social implications. Some countries responded more quickly and aggressively to the COVID-19 pandemic, which is reflected in the death rate. For example, Sweden followed a herd mentality model and did not lock down their economy. As a result, Sweden has had one of the highest death rates from COVID-19 in the developed world per percentage of the total population. Other countries like New Zealand took a more hardline approach with a strict lockdown policy that resulted in significantly lower death rates than other countries. The different possible ways of reacting to the COVID-19 pandemic have created debate due to the need to balance social priorities with economic goals. Governments have responded to the need to take urgent action with a warlike mentality. This has meant the usages of the word 'fight' in language about the COVID-19 pandemic, which is similar to that used in times of military conflict. The militaristic language is common in times of crisis due to the need to respond promptly to change (Branicki, 2020). This is due to crisis managers taking a strategic approach that emphasizes critical action.

Small businesses during the COVID-19 crisis need to develop their resilience. Martin and Sunley (2015) suggest that regional economic resilience is based on (1) industrial and business structure, (2) labor market conditions, (3) agency and decision-making, (4) financial arrangements, and (5) governance arrangements. Industrial and business structure refers to the types of industries located in a region and their ability to respond in times of crisis. This depends on whether there is a diverse array of business or if they are specialized around certain industries. The market orientation of the businesses in terms of domestic and/or international will also influence their level of resilience. The business level of entrepreneurial orientation in terms of innovation, risk-taking and proactiveness also needs to be examined. This will help to understand the debt structure and financial strength of the business. The labor market conditions refer to the skills and educational qualifications. Some regions will have workers with more occupational flexibility that is useful in times of crisis. The reality for many small businesses particularly in the tourism and high contact service industry is no customers and being unable to operate. This causes extreme hardship and much uncertainty. It is becoming harder to keep a small business afloat during the COVID-19 crisis.

There are a number of ways to mitigate risk during the COVID-19 crisis by encouraging a resilience approach including through active mediation, managing alertness, and by navigating the environment. Active mediation involves meeting with other stakeholders to assess risks. This enables information to be shared among a diverse group of entities. By discussing with others their assessment of risks it enables a better understanding of the changes required. This communication is essential in managing the advantages and disadvantages of risk. Moreover, as risk varies over a period of time, it can help to gain feedback from others about its impact. This can enable a more holistic understanding about environmental impacts of the risk. Managing alertness means complying with changing regulations regarding risk. As risk can involve financial and social impact it can help to be alert to new developments. This enables small businesses to quickly pivot based on need. Part of this process involves monitoring risk to see how it changes based on market developments. Navigating the environment means finding new paths to take based on changes in demand and supply. Risk impacts individuals differently depending on their position in society. This means business leaders will be more in favor of certain causes of action based on their perceived impact of the risk. To develop an efficient risk mitigation strategy, small business owners need to obtain a thorough understanding of market change.

The COVID crisis has meant more market change and attention is being placed on public health systems to treat patients but also contain growth. The rapidly unfolding events derived from COVID-19 have meant substantial changes to current ways of living and working. Small businesses have different levels of preparedness for crises and for many small businesses the resulting social changes from COVID-19 were unexpected. The rapid impact of COVID-19 has meant businesses need to update their responses on a frequent basis. There is also a lot of speculation about the ramifications of COVID-19 on society and the economy in general. This is due to the confusion about the facts of the virus and how it has spread in the community. In addition, each country has taken a different approach.

Most small businesses are encountering an array of challenges in terms of how to respond to the COVID-19 crisis. The importance of digital technology has become visible due to the need for small businesses to respond to customer needs. The COVID-19 crisis has been a brutal disruption to small business and necessitated a quick change. Global supply chains for small businesses have become a liability in light of travel restrictions. This has meant a need to look more local for the sourcing and supply of goods. The impossibility of maintaining in-person transactions in the tourism and hospitality industry has led to the near collapse of many small businesses. The long-term effects of the COVID-19 crisis for small businesses are still unknown, but it is increasingly becoming evident in the short term that more digital capabilities are required in order to survive.

The implementation of prevention methods, such as lockdowns, quarantines, and social distancing, has challenged small businesses. The International Monetary Fund predicts that the COVID-19 crisis will be worse than the 2008 global financial crisis (Kang et al., 2020). To respond to the COVID-19 crisis, small business managers can change their product development process to adjust products to meet emerging market needs. This helps to build a capacity for changing environmental circumstances that cannot be predicted through normal scenario planning. To do this, small business managers need to coordinate their supply chains through migrating to a digital platform. This can enable better customer relationship management processes to develop that focus on specific market needs utilizing entrepreneurial digital transformation processes.

Entrepreneurship and digital transformation

There is no universally preferred of entrepreneurship in the literature, which means there are a number of different ways to define the concept. Typically an entrepreneurship definition will mention risk and innovation, which are considered essential features of entrepreneurship. Some definitions will discuss the context in which the entrepreneurship takes place. Kasabov (2016:682) defines entrepreneurship as 'developing new ventures outside existing organizations, involving "risk taking," "innovation" and a "proactive strategic emphasis."' Another definition by Maden (2015:313) states, 'entrepreneurship has become a term that is increasingly widespread around the world, as it is closely associated with economic development and wellbeing of societies.' Thus, the role entrepreneurship plays in times of the COVID-19 crisis has attracted the attention of key players in society. Although entrepreneurship plays an important role in the global economy, our knowledge is limited to normally noncrisis moments. This means that most entrepreneurship theory is based on stable environmental conditions. This limits our understanding of how crisis situations affect entrepreneurship.

Brush, de Bruin and Welter (2009:9) state, 'current entrepreneurship theory explaining venture creation is generally organised around three basic constructs, namely market, money and management.' Markets are essential to entrepreneurs due to the need to sell products and/or services. Markets can differ in nature based on the type of transaction and level of economic development. Formal markets require regulation by governments and are governed by specific policies. Informal markets tend to be less regulated and based on trust. Entrepreneurs are motivated by money in their need to enter markets. This means they need to manage their business activities in order to ensure successful outcomes.

The presence of entrepreneurship in society during the COVID-19 crisis is assumed to be built on long-lasting relationships. This assumption might not be correct due to the need for sudden and forceful types of entrepreneurship being needed due to COVID-19 restrictions. While a stakeholder perspective is ingrained in more definitions of entrepreneurship, the actions of stakeholders might change in times of crisis (Ratten and Ferreira, 2017). This means new knowledge related to how internal and external actors respond to crises like the COVID-19 pandemic is required. This enables a better understanding about the accrual of distinctive social capital in times of massive change. Entrepreneurship does not occur in a vacuum but is based on trusting relationships that enable business ventures to be built (Ratten and Dana, 2015). Highly intensive communications regarding business ventures might be needed because of COVID-19 changes. This means the management of value chains is based on context and suitability. While digital solutions have enabled entrepreneurs to continue operating during and after lockdown, they also change the nature of business relationships due to the omission of physical human contact (Ratten, 2016).

The unexpected demand for digital services was known but the way it has occurred in the marketplace due to COVID-19 restrictions was not planned (Reeves, Lang and Carlsson-Szlezak, 2020). Such disruptions have caused entrepreneurs to rethink existing business models and to develop new ideas about future growth trajectories (Saarikko, Westergren and Blomquist, 2020). This means entrepreneurship research should stress more the positive and negative results arising from the COVID-19 pandemic. By complementing existing research and practice on digital transformation, entrepreneurship researchers can further develop related studies. This can involve considering in more depth heterogeneous types of entrepreneurship that previously were not considered (Qian, 2018). This means delving into the mechanisms and implications of a sudden shift toward digital technology. An intensified focus on digital technology in the context of COVID-19 is likely to alter the way entrepreneurship is studied. This includes changing belief patterns about the goals and motivations of entrepreneurs in society. Scholars need to urgently address what constitutes successful entrepreneurship in the COVID-19 environment in terms of financial and social outcomes. This can include analyzing how planned and unplanned forms of COVID-19 entrepreneurship occur and under which environmental contexts entrepreneurship is more likely to occur.

There will always be inefficiencies in the market so it is the job of an entrepreneur to find them. This can be difficult depending on the existing economic conditions. Entrepreneurs try to disrupt markets by employing innovative techniques. To do this means intentionally developing a business with the idea of filling a market need. This process means creating a business venture that disrupts current market practices (Simao and Franco, 2018).

Most thinking in the area of entrepreneurship involves focusing on the process of identifying and exploiting opportunities. A small business tends to operate with limited resources based on being close to the customer. Many small businesses are family-owned and are passed down generations but not all small businesses are the same as they differ in terms of market share and industry structure.

Despite the rapidly growing literature on COVID-19 entrepreneurship, there is an inconsistent use of the term that results in no additional value to the scholarly discourse. The vague way COVID-19 entrepreneurship is defined means that there is a lack of clear direction about its meaning. There is an overwhelming amount of support for the use of entrepreneurship in times of crisis. Academic, industry, policy practitioners, and managers are recognizing the value of entrepreneurship to the solving of problems caused by the COVID-19 pandemic. This is particularly relevant in the way entrepreneurs utilize social media for digital transformation.

Social media and digital transformation

Social media is a type of digital media that is being used to communicate messages about the COVID-19 pandemic. The growing use of social media is due to the way it can quickly convey messages to society. This means the flow of information occurs more swiftly than traditional marketing communication methods (Uitdewilligen and Waller, 2018). In addition, social media provides a form of collective communication that is helpful in building a sense of community. This enables a broader audience to be reached through retweets. Retweeting enables additional information to be added to the initial post. Thereby continuing the conversation in real time based on interactive communication. This also enables more contextual information based on updated conditions to be included. Governments and crisis response officials are utilizing social media because of its transformational capability to convey important information.

In the digital marketplace, consumers are using more interactive tools to make purchase decisions. This has led to an increase in mobile communications that operate in real time. The explosion of growth in the amount of online data available has given rise to the data analytics field. Data if analyzed in the right way can be used by businesses to further their growth strategies. Customers are making purchase decision based on social media in which information is shared (Ratten, Dana and Ramandani, 2015). Social media has spearheaded the virtual revolution due to increased levels of connectivity by organizations rethinking their purpose in the COVID-19 environment.

Organizations that clearly articulate their purpose generally have more favorable outcomes in terms of commitment and motivation of employees. Silard (2018:306) describes an organizational purpose as 'a highly motivating mechanisms through which leaders motivate followers, sometimes even more influential than financial gain.' The purpose of an organization can vary depending on the intent of leaders and the industry characteristics (Tajeddini, Altinay and Ratten, 2017). Hollensbe, Wookey, Hickey, George and Nichols (2014:1228) define an organizational purpose as 'the reason for which business is created or exists, its meaning and direction.' Organizations need to articulate their purpose in order to create more value-adding behaviors. This can be a challenge since organizational leaders need to focus on emerging digital entrepreneurship environmental conditions.

Digital entrepreneurship in the COVID-19 crisis

Digital innovation refers to new processes or platforms being used in a digital context. This involves a concerted effort to bring in new technology that utilizes digital representation (Audretsch, Cunningham, Kuratko, Lehmann and Menter, 2019). Innovation involves a process of turning an idea into a marketable product or service. This means it is more than just invention as it involves commercialization. Therefore, innovation has a business element as it involves economic activity. The business element is evident in the way ideas emerge in the economy and then are implemented into business practices. Entrepreneurs are innovators as they produce change in the marketplace. This change is instrumental in providing services and products to fit market gaps. Entrepreneurs establish businesses with the goal of obtaining a profit but do so in an innovative manner.

Fast-changing market environments require the use of technological innovation in order to maintain competitive momentum. This means technology in the form of new knowledge provides a way for businesses to compete based on entrepreneurship. The entrepreneurship process for small businesses is different. This is due to the dominant role being the owner compared to delegated management control in large companies. This means in large companies' decisions are made by a board of directors looking after shareholder interests. This can mean large businesses have more time and resources to make decisions. This can be a good and bad thing depending on the context. Small businesses can act in a more flexible and nimble way because they do not have to report to stakeholders. This means they can act quickly and obtain market advantages before others. However, small businesses can be resource-constricted meaning they might not have financial or human capital to pursue opportunities. Thus, large firms that have resource abundance can obtain better economies of scale. This can also lead to more international expansion in the marketplace. Although not all large companies can pursue opportunities due to bureaucratic rigidity meaning each decision has to be evaluated on the basis of merit. This can slow progression due to the need to think about alternative business possibilities.

Entrepreneurship research is built on a tradition of incorporating interdisciplinary perspectives that involve some form of creativity. Creativity is defined as 'the production of novel and useful ideas by an individual or small group of individuals working together' (Amabile, 1996:1155). There are four main factors for understanding creativity in individuals: (1) personality, (2) intrinsic motivation, (3) knowledge, and (4) cognitive skills and abilities (Dimov, 2007). Small businesses that have a strong online presence are likely to do better than those who do not during the COVID-19 crisis. Small businesses can alter their strategies to fit the new environmental conditions by refocusing their market orientation. This means assessing their target market based on buying patterns. This involves digital marketing analytics that provides better insights.

Normally when an organization wants to reinvigorate its business operations, it will decide to utilize an entrepreneurial approach. An entrepreneurial strategy is defined as 'the means through which an organisation establishes and re-establishes its fundamental set of relationships with the environment' (Murray, 1984:1). This enables new actions to be taken that change current modes of operation. The creation of an entrepreneurial strategy can take time to develop as it must be innovative. The COVID-19 crisis threatens the existence of many small businesses around the world. While the government interventions in the form of enforced homeworking are needed, they significantly affect the viability of many small businesses. The unintended consequences of these government restrictions have been a change in the way many small businesses are conducted. Governments have responded to the COVID-19 crisis in different ways with some countries most notably Sweden avoiding lockdowns and keeping their businesses open. Other countries have taken aggressive action to stop the spread of the virus by mandating business closures or altering existing practices.

The small business market is not only a highly competitive space but also an industry with a strong global presence. The small business sector comprises a number of diverse industries including manufacturing, hospitality, and tourism. However, small business represents a sector with prolific growth but also is susceptible to market events. In order to respond to crises, small business managers are confronted with significant logistics challenges with operations being affected in different ways. Although small businesses management has become a prevalent research topic in the entrepreneurship discipline, researchers are only now starting to understand the effects of COVID-19. In fact, so far there has been no concentrated effort in outlining the strategic relevance of COVID-19 to the small business sector. This is due to researchers being shy to acknowledge the area of COVID-19 in small business management. While COVID-19 is a popular topic particularly in terms of small business response, there is a lack of adequate research on the topic. The absence of engagement with logistical aspects of small business is not justified, given the impact, small business has on the economy. It appears that there is still much to learn about small business and the role they place in responding to the COVID-19 crisis.

Small businesses have begun to catch up with large businesses in terms of developing innovative capabilities. Small businesses try to be innovative thinking they can simply modify the research and development skills used by large businesses. However, while there are several examples of successful innovation transfers from large to small businesses, there usually needs to be some kind of adaptation to suit the small business context. Small businesses are now encountering a need for innovation because of the effects of COVID-19. Over the past year, small businesses have had to survive while maintaining an innovation orientation.

Disruption in sport social media

In disrupting previous marketing models, social media have served to bridge an ever-increasing gap between the expense of live fandom and free expansive exposure, creating a new form of fandom which takes advantage of the digital age. Within the industry, the proliferation of social media has been driven by various stakeholders such as professional sport teams, leagues, professional athletes, professional sporting events, and sport fans. Indeed, more and more, sport fans are taken in by the power of social media and demand connections within the digital space. From a relationship marketing standpoint, social media have transformed the way in which relationships between fans and sport organizations are developed and maintained. Essentially, this disruption has presented an opportunity for sport organizations to reach almost every customer in real time to engage in dialogue with them, and to create, in due course, a mutually valued product.

Social media research has shown that they are valuable digital marketing communication tools, with benefits including, but not limited to, developing social connections, direct communication of brand image, and enhanced loyalty (Thompson, Martin, Gee and Geurin, 2018). Importantly, one of the key marketing benefits of social media are the opportunities they present for positive brand-building endeavors (Thompson, Martin, Gee and Geurin, 2016) as use of these digital platforms can affect consumer perceptions, and potentially influence consumptive behaviors (Thompson et al., 2016). Thus, organizations that fail to successfully engage in this digital space may see a loss of fans, competitive advantage, and the benefits that social media provide.

Digital sport marketing examples

The London 2012 Olympic Games were dubbed the first ever truly digital Games, and the way sport is packaged and marketed to its consumers has undoubtedly changed since due to digital marketing. Importantly, sport organizations seeking to leverage digital marketing opportunities should focus on engaging sport fans. Their focus needs to shift from simply filling a stadium with fans to engaging specific groups of fans both inside and outside a venue, throughout preseason, successful and unsuccessful years, and postseasons.

Wimbledon, a storied and traditionalist institution, replete with its tournament stalwarts, banks on social media to reach, and engage with fans to build their brand and relationships with them. Working with technology partner IBM, Wimbledon has used IBM Watson Content Analytics and artificial intelligence to create enriched fan experiences. Using technology that provides insights into social conversations, the tournament launched 'Hill versus the World.' Fans sitting on Wimbledon's Henman Hill were asked questions on the big screen, while those following from around the world had the same questions posed to them on social media. Responses were then tracked to show the difference in sentiment and engagement between the audience on the hill in the ground versus the audience in the rest of the World. In another example, this technology has also been central to the Watson-enabled chatbot, 'Ask Fred' designed to reinvent how fans experience the tournament, with the cognitive assistant answering a range of questions from fans visiting the event. They have also continued to offer enhanced mobile app products to enhance the fan experience with customized content filters, personalized order of play, natural language interface, and interactive venue maps.

Search engine optimization (SEO) has taken on significant prominence within the sport industry and has been used to enhance exposure and generate additional website traffic. Many organizations including retailers and professionals such as personal trainers and fitness coaches, nutritionists, and psychologists have developed SEO strategies to optimize their prominence within search engine results to enhance click through rates. Organizations are also using SEO for brand management to ensure that positive (on-brand) listings are presented within the results. As negative publicity can be damaging to a brand, it is prudent to limit exposure to search content in search results. For example, during a time when the Australian cricket team received significant negative press and online coverage during a ball-tampering scandal involving several national players, search results for 'Australian cricket team' were positive.

As noted earlier, video marketing has emerged as an innovative part of digital marketing. Many sport organizations have turned to content and video marketing strategies, featuring unique content which has been optimized for digital audiences. This offers sport entities benefits associated with building brand awareness, enhancing fan engagement, and driving traffic to official websites. Social live streaming services have emerged as an extension of video marketing that should be incorporated within a sport organization's digital marketing strategy. As COVID-19 spread around the world in the early part of 2020, its impact on the professional sports industry was profound as tournaments, games, and other sporting events were postponed or canceled. During this period, live streaming provided an opportunity to forge closer connections with audiences and also one of the few ways to share new content with fans (Wymer and Thompson, 2020).

While virtual and augmented reality use in sport is still in its infancy, there are several examples of teams that are integrating this technology into their digital marketing toolkit to create immersive experiences for local and global audiences, inside and outside stadiums. With respect to virtual reality, in 2017, FC Bayern Munich allowed fans to virtually create selfies with star players within its app. In 2020, amid crowd-less NBA playoff games due to COVID-19, fans were invited to watch the game, in real time, through livestream. This initiative also came to the attention of celebrities such as Lil Wayne, who gave the fan 'next' to him a cyber high five during a Lakers game. Sports Illustrated (n.d.) used augmented and virtual reality technology to allow people to experience a bottom-to-top climb of Mount Everest, the world's highest mountain. Users who downloaded the LIFE VR app to see this could also explore the first augmented reality issue featuring additional multimedia content. As a marketing tool, this worked to showcase *Sports Illustrated*'s access and storytelling ability while also providing an innovative example of how print publications could remain relevant in the digital era. This technology also enables sport organizations to virtually replace in-stadia advertising during a live broadcast, allowing sport marketers to optimize and target adds to in-stadia and at-home viewers and provide geo-targeted advertising content to global audiences. For example, during a friendly match between England and Costa Rica in 2018, Virtual Replacement Technology was used to present dynamic perimeter ads to streaming audiences who were split into two feeds: one to the Americas and another one to Asia, Australasia, and parts of Europe (Sports Business Daily, 2018). As sport organizations continue to delve further into augmented reality, there are significant opportunities for teams and leagues to develop advertising activations that move beyond static content.

In terms of customization, the Los Angeles organizing committee for the 2028 Summer Olympics has unveiled interchangeable official logos in an innovative twist on the traditional approach. While the 'L,' '2,' and '8' are static across all versions, variations have been applied to the 'A' in order to reflect 'the city's diversity and allow for dynamism over the eight-year run-up to the Games' (Smith, 2020). While these initial logos will be available on all official merchandize, fans will also have the ability to design their own customized version of the LA28 logo. Moreover, it is important for organizations to acknowledge the need for their digital marketing practices, and strategy, to be consistent with their broader marketing imperatives. That is, there needs to be a digital 'line of sight' that connects all plans and activities within the organization.

Conclusion

To conclude, further thought is required about the digital transformations of small businesses because of the COVID-19 crisis. Digital technology plays a pervasive role in shaping economic efficiency during a crisis. COVID-19 entrepreneurship is significantly different from general entrepreneurship, so an adaptation of existing theories is required. Context influences the dynamics of new venture creation and entrepreneurship. A crucial contextual influence on entrepreneurship is the COVID-19 crisis. This is reflected in burgeoning empirical research showing that small business entrepreneurial activities have been fundamentally shaped by the COVID-19 crisis. At the moment, theory is underdeveloped and lacking with regard to how small businesses have been influenced by the COVID-19 crisis. Theory building around COVID-19 is likely to attract more attention due to the unique way COVID-19 has influenced entrepreneurial processes. Entrepreneurship is now of the main drivers of innovation and is an essential element of economic development. Small businesses are the backbone of the economy and affect the well-being of society. The success of entrepreneurship depends largely on the ability of small businesses to adapt to change. The strength of small business lies in enabling knowledge and learning opportunities. During the COVID-19 crisis, access to knowledge is being facilitated by digital technology. Therefore, as discussed in this chapter, it is crucial that small businesses embed an entrepreneurial strategy to utilize more digital technology. This will enable a more holistic digital transformation that can help small businesses compete in the global marketplace.

References

Amabile, T. M. (1996) *Creativity and innovation in organizations* (Vol. 5). Boston, MA: Harvard Business School.

Anggadwita, G., Ramadani, V., Alamanda, D., Ratten, V. and Hashani, M. (2016) 'Entrepreneurial intention from Islamic perspective: A study of Muslim entrepreneurs in Indonesia', *International Journal of Entrepreneurship and Small Business*, 31(2): 165–179.

Audretsch, D., Cunningham, J., Kuratko, D., Lehmann, E. and Menter, M. (2019) 'Entrepreneurial ecosystems: Economic, technological and societal impacts', *The Journal of Technology Transfer*, 44: 313–325.

Branicki, L. (2020) 'Covid-19, ethics of care and feminist crisis management', *Gender, Work and Organization*, 27: 872–883.

Brush, C. G., de Bruin, A. and Welter, F. (2009) 'A gender-aware framework for women's entrepreneurship', *International Journal of Gender and Entrepreneurship*, 1(1): 8–24.

Dalmarco, G., Ramalho, F. R., Barros, A. C. and Soares, A. L. (2019) 'Providing industry 4.0 technologies: The case of a production technology cluster', *The Journal of High Technology Management Research*, 30(2): 1–9.

Dimov, D. (2007) 'Beyond the single-person single-insight attribution in understanding entrepreneurial opportunities', *Entrepreneurship Theory & Practice*, September: 713–731.

Ferreira, J., Fernandes, C., Peris-Ortiz, M. and Ratten, V. (2017) 'Female entrepreneurship: A co-citation analysis', *International Journal of Entrepreneurship and Small Business*, 31(2): 325–340.

Ferreira, J., Ratten, V. and Dana, L. (2017) 'Knowledge based spillovers and strategic entrepreneurship', *International Entrepreneurship and Management Journal*, 13(1): 161–167.

Gomez, S., Mendoza, O., Ramirez, J. and Olivas-Lujan, M. (2020) 'Stress and myths related to the Covid-19 pandemic's effects on remote work', *Management Research: Journal of the Iberoamerican Academy of Management*, 18(4): 401–420.

Hinings, B., Gegenhuber, T. and Greenwood, R. (2018) 'Digital innovation and transformation: An institutional perspective', *Information and Organization*, 28: 52–61.

Hollensbe, E., Wookey, C., Hickey, L., George, G. and Nichols, N. (2014) 'Organizations with purpose', *Academy of Management Journal*, 57: 1227–1234.

Kang, J., Diao, Z. and Zanini, M. (2020) 'Business-to-business marketing responses to Covid-19 crisis: A business process perspective', *Marketing Intelligence & Planning*, In Press.

Kasabov, E. (2016) 'When an initiative promises more than it delivers: A multi-actor per-spective of rural entrepreneurship difficulties and failure in Thailand', *Entrepreneurship & Regional Development*, 28(9–10): 681–703.

Maden, C. (2015) 'A gendered lens on entrepreneurship: Women entrepreneurship in Tur-key', *Gender in Management: An International Journal*, 30(4): 312–331.

Martin, R. and Sunley, P. (2015) 'On the notion of regional economic resilience: Concep-tualization and explanation', *Journal of Economic Geography*, 15(1): 1–42.

Murray, J. (1984) 'A concept of entrepreneurial strategy', *Strategic Management Journal*, 5: 1–13.

Qian, H. (2018) 'Knowledge-based regional economic development: A synthetic review of knowledge spillovers, entrepreneurship and entrepreneurial ecosystems', *Economic Develop-ment Quarterly*, 32(2): 163–176.

Ratten, V. (2014) 'Indian and US consumer purchase intentions of cloud computing ser-vices', *Journal of Indian Business Research*, 6(2): 170–188.

Ratten, V. (2015) 'A cross-cultural comparison of online behavioural advertising knowledge, online privacy concerns and social networking using the technology acceptance model and social cognitive theory', *Journal of Science and Technology Policy Management*, 6(1): 25–36.

Ratten, V. (2016) 'Continuance use intention of cloud computing: Innovativeness and cre-ativity perspectives', *Journal of Business Research*, 69(5): 1737–1740.

Ratten, V. and Dana, L.-P. (2015) 'Indigenous food entrepreneurship in Australia: Mark Olive 'Australia's Jamie Oliver' and Indigiearth', *International Journal of Entrepreneurship and Small Business*, 26(3): 265–279.

Ratten, V., Dana, L.-P. and Ramadani, V. (2015) 'Internationalisation of family business groups in transition economies', *International Journal of Entrepreneurship and Small Business*, 30(4): 509–525.

Ratten, V. and Ferreira, J. (2017) 'Future research directions for cultural entrepreneurship and regional innovation', *International Journal of Entrepreneurship and Innovation*, 21(3): 163–169.

Reeves, M., Lang, N. and Carlsson-Szlezak, P. (2020) 'Lead your business through the coronavirus crisis', *Harvard Business Review*, In Press.

Saarikko, T., Westergren, U. and Blomquist, T. (2020) 'Digital transformation: Five recom-mendations for the digitally conscious firm', *Business Horizons*, 63: 825–839.

Santos, G., Marques, C., Ferreira, J., Gerry, C. and Ratten, V. (2017) 'Women's entrepre-neurship in Northern Portugal: Psychological factors versus contextual influences in the economic downturn', *World Review of Entrepreneurship, Management and Sustainable Develop-ment*, 13(4): 418–440.

SchWeber, C. (2013) 'Survival lessons: Academic continuity, business continuity, and tech-nology', In *Facilitating learning in the 21st century: Leading through technology, diversity and authenticity* (pp. 151–163). Dordrecht: Springer.

Silard, A. (2018) 'Emotions for a cause: How the emotion expression of non-profit leaders produces follower engagement and loyalty', *Nonprofit and Voluntary Sector Quarterly*, 47(2): 304–324.

Simao, L. and Franco, M. (2018) 'External knowledge sources as antecedents of organiza-tional innovation in firm workplaces: A knowledge-based perspective', *Journal of Knowledge Management*, In Press.

Smith, C. (2020) *LA28 launches official logos for Olympics Games*, 1st September 2020, www.sportsbusinessdaily.com/SB-Blogs/Breaking-News/2020/08/LA28-Logos.aspx

Sports Business Daily (2018) *FA, ITV test virtually augmented advertising technology*, 14th June 2018, www.sportsbusinessdaily.com/Global/Issues/2018/06/14/Media/ITV-FA.aspx

Sports Illustrated. (n.d.). *Capturing Everest: A ground-breaking VR experience*, www.si.com/specials/everest-climb-virtual-reality/index.html

Tajeddini, K., Altinay, L. and Ratten, V. (2017) 'Service innovativeness and the structuring of organizations: The moderating roles of learning orientation and inter-functional coordination', *International Journal of Hospitality Management*, 65: 100–114.

Thompson, A., Martin, A. J., Gee, S. and Geurin, A. N. (2016) 'Fans' perceptions of professional tennis events' social media presence: Interaction, insight, and brand anthropomorphism', *Communication & Sport*, 5(5). https://doi.org/10.1177/2167479516650442.

Thompson, A., Martin, A. J., Gee, S. and Geurin, A. N. (2018) 'Building brand and fan relationships through social media', *Sport, Business and Management: An International Journal*, 8(3): 235–256.

Uitdewilligen, S. and Waller, M. (2018) 'Information sharing and decision-making in multidisciplinary crisis management teams', *Journal of Organizational Behaviour*, 39: 731–748.

Venkatesh, V. (2020) 'Impacts of Covid-19: A research agenda to support people in their fight', *International Journal of Information Management*, In Press.

Vial, G. (2019) 'Understanding digital transformation: A review and research agenda', *Journal of Strategic Information Systems*, 28: 118–144.

Wymer, S. and Thompson, A. (2020) 'Diminishing the distance during social distancing: An exploration of Australian sport organisations' usage of social live streaming services throughout Covid-19', In P. M. Pedersen, B. J. Ruihley, and B. Li (Eds.), *Sport and the pandemic: Perspectives on Covid-19's impact on the sport industry* (pp. 61–69). London: Routledge.

6 The impact of the experiences on affects during the COVID-19 pandemic quarantine

Eulália Santos, Ana Diogo, Vanessa Ratten, and Fernando Tavares

Introduction

The World Health Organization (2011) defined health not only as the absence of disease but also as a state of physical, mental, and social well-being. Thus, the concept of well-being has a high importance in the lives of individuals and companies. According to some authors, the terms happiness and well-being are considered synonymous (Diener and Ryan, 2009; Satuf, Monteiro, Pereira, Esgalhado, Afonso and Loureiro, 2018). For Ferraz, Tavares and Zilberman (2007), happiness is a positive emotional state that results in feelings of well-being and pleasure, while for Keyes, Shmotkin and Ryff (2002) happiness is the result of the balance between positive affect and negative affect.

The human being, since he is born and throughout his life, follows a path full of experiences, some pleasant and others unpleasant, in which the temperament and the environment in which he lives influences his happiness (Kesebir and Diener, 2008).

The COVID-19 pandemic is a serious problem facing the world and humanity, since the SARS-CoV-2 virus circulates around the world. This virus started in China in December 2019 (Huang, Wang, Li, Ren, Zhao, Hu and Cheng, 2020), and since then until July 23, 2020, it has infected more than 15 million people worldwide and was the cause of the death of more than 630,000 (Worldometers, 2020).

The governments of the vast majority of countries in the world decided, more or less quickly, to adopt quarantine as a measure of containment. Quarantine completely changed people's lifestyles and daily lives, preventing them from moving freely. Thus, because of all the changes that the quarantine forced, it becomes pertinent to relate the experiences of individuals with the affects. Portugal was chosen to carry out the present study, as there are no known quarantine reports in the last 100 years and for having adopted the quarantine right at the beginning of the pandemic outbreak, that is, on March 18 (16 days after being detected the first case) when there were only 642 infected and 2 deaths (Worldometers, 2020).

The present study aims to study the impact of experiences on affects during the COVID-19 pandemic quarantine. The article is structured in four parts.

In the introduction, the problem under analysis and its relevance are defined, and the objectives of the study are presented. In the literature review section, the concepts of affects and the experiences lived during the quarantine are addressed, as well as the relationship between these two concepts, ending this section with the formulation of the hypotheses. In the materials and methods section, the sample is presented and the procedures performed during data collection are explained, the measurement instrument used is described, and this section ends with a description of the analytical methods used. In the results and discussion section, the respondents' sociodemographic characterization and the measurement model are presented, and the hypotheses are tested using the structural model. In order to facilitate reading, the discussion is presented together with the results. Finally, the conclusions with the main results, implications, and proposals for future investigations are presented.

Literature review

Affects

Positive psychology is dedicated to the study of the virtues and human potential, where well-being is one of the major areas of research (Ivtzan, Lomas, Hefferon and Worth, 2015; Seligman and Csikszentmihalyi, 2000). Regarding well-being, two approaches stand out: subjective well-being and psychological well-being. Subjective well-being is defined as a combination of high satisfaction with life, high positive affect, and low negative affect (Diener, 2000), that is, it presupposes the occurrence of frequent experiences of positive affects and infrequent negative affects (Harris, Daniels and Briner, 2003; Noronha, Delforno and Pinto, 2014). The concept of psychological well-being refers to human development in overcoming the existential challenges of life, contemplating various dimensions of psychological functioning (Keyes et al., 2002).

Affects (positive and negative) constitute the affective dimension of the concept of subjective well-being (Diener and Larsen, 1984). For Cohen, Pham and Andrade (2008), affects refer to an internal emotional state related to a certain emotion. In this sense, positive affects involve fun and satisfaction with life (Diener, Pressman, Hunter and Delgadillo-Chase, 2017) and negative affects involve states related to anger and worry, but also involve feelings such as depression (Diener et al., 2017).

Galinha, Pereira and Esteves (2014), in the development of a reduced Portuguese version of the scale of positive and negative affects, concluded that the variables with greater weight in positive affects were enthusiasm, inspired, delighted, warm, and determined, and the variables with greater weight in the negative affects were scared, frightened, tormented, disturbed, and nervous. Well-being is not only studied in the individual domain but also can have influences from the context surrounding the individual, that is, it can have influence from family, work, community, and society (La Placa, McNaught and Knight, 2013).

Happiness at work is closely related to the individual's subjective well-being, revealing how people are or are not satisfied with their work and life, being crucial when aiming at improving productivity in any type of organization (Wesarat, Sharif and Majid, 2015). Thus, the work context presents itself as a privileged place of emotions and achievement and construction of personal happiness (Paschoal and Tamayo, 2008).

In the work context, in the literature review, there are also scales that assess the affects (Ferreira, Correa, Fernandes and Almeida, 2008; Gouveia, Fonsêca, Lins, Lima and Gouveia, 2008; Paschoal and Tamayo, 2008). The scales of Ferreira et al. (2008) and Gouveia et al. (2008) are composed by the dimensions, positive and negative affect, and the scale of Paschoal and Tamayo (2008) analyzes the well-being at work, being constituted by three dimensions, the positive affect, the negative affect, and the achievement in the job.

The determination of quarantine as a measure of containment, in addition to changing lifestyles, also changed behaviors and psychologically impacted individuals (Desclaux, Badji, Ndione and Sow, 2017).

Experiences

Experience is defined as a subjective construction and individual transformation, where emotions and feelings stand out (Grundey, 2008), being considered a fundamental element in marketing, as it interferes with how the individual feels, knows, or does things (Same and Larimo, 2012).

According to Schmitt (1999), experiences are events that can be the real or virtual result of direct observation or participation in a given event. This author introduced into the literature five strategic experiential marketing modules called Strategic Experiential Modules (SEMs), which are based on customer experiences: Sense, Feel, Think, Act, and Relate. These modules have been addressed in the literature giving rise to some studies (Kao, Huang and Wu, 2008; Lee and Chang, 2012; Santos, Santos, Caldeira, Oliveira and Miguel, 2019; Tsaur, Chiu and Wang, 2007; Wu and Tseng, 2014). In the context of this study, the strategic experimental modules by Schmitt (1999) are the different types of experiences that individuals experience during the quarantine period, the consumers of the experiences are the individuals and the experience itself can be analyzed as the brand or the company.

Agapito, Mendes, Valle and Almeida (2014) consider that sensory marketing offers an important contribution to the marketing of experiences, since the five senses of people (sight, hearing, smell, taste, and touch) are responsible for processing the sensory stimuli present in the external environment, physical or virtual, triggering the different sensations. Thus, through the senses, the human being can perceive a set of information about the environment in which he lives, in particular, the situation experienced in the quarantine.

Family bonds and interaction are very important in the formation of children, and family relationships are based on the first affective bonds, which are an essential element for human survival (Esteves and Ribeiro, 2016). Affective relationships have a crucial role in the formation of human intelligence, being built throughout the process of the development of an individual, providing meaning to the experiences and the needs he has throughout life (Wallon, 1979). Emotions also play a fundamental role in survival and well-being (Tooby and Cosmides, 2008), these being considered by Scherer (2005) responses that adapt to environmental stimuli, involving changes in subjective experience, as well as in other domains (cognitive, motivational, physiological, and behavioral).

Individuals who experience positive affect most often are those who are most satisfied with life, who have the most positive expectations for the future and who have the highest self-esteem (Wong and Lim, 2009; Zanon, Bastianello, Pacico and Hutz, 2013), which, combined with imagination, is essential for creativity (Santos, Gibim and Wechsler, 2020). In this way, you can promote well-being and reduce negative stress (Nakano, Machado and Abreu, 2019). According to Corrêa and Gouvêa (2019), creativity generates experiences of thinking, living, and feeling that are transformed into real, concrete, and positive changes in society.

As for Same and Larimo (2012), the experiences can result in changes in the consumer's attitude or behavior, cognitively (mental images, interpretation, and understanding), affective (feelings and emotions), and conative (intentions and actions). After quarantine, people also change their behavior, for example, avoiding joining large crowds and changing hygiene behaviors (Cava, Fay, Beanlands, McCay and Wignall, 2005).

Experiences and affects

Due to the central role that affects play in the experience of human life (Gray and Watson, 2007), it is important to study their relationship between affects and experiences. Each person's reaction to circumstances is reflected in each moment, positively or negatively. Even though there are changes in emotions depending on the circumstances that the individual faces along the way, he has emotional responses characteristic of a variety of situations and circumstances in life (Diener, Lucas and Oishi, 2005).

According to Van Horn, Taris, Schaufeli and Scheurs (2004), affects can be characterized by the frequency of feelings and emotions. Positive affects include the various feelings that individuals experience when situations are favorable, while negative affects include feelings resulting from unfavorable experiences. For Soraggi and Paschoal (2011), in a context that offers possibilities for autonomy, creative thinking, recognition and social prestige, the worker's happiness, and his well-being at work significantly increase.

The results of the study by Hirschle, Gondim, Alberton and Ferreira (2019) allow us to infer that if the worker understands that there are more effective ways of dealing with positive or negative situations at work, he will be able to preserve his work well-being. For these authors, the perception of stress makes it difficult for the worker to use strategies that prolong the benefits of positive affects (adaptive strategies) triggered by favorable situations in the work environment, reducing their well-being. Once the individual perceives a stressful environment, he seems to have difficulties in using more appropriate strategies for different scenarios, adopting nonadaptive and dysfunctional strategies. In this way, not knowing how to regulate the effects of negative emotions is detrimental to well-being. In order to reduce the frequency and intensity of negative affective experiences, it is important for the worker to participate in activities that involve social contact with colleagues, such as work gymnastics, relaxation moments, and celebrating the birthdays of coworkers (Couto and Paschoal, 2017).

Taking into account the study objectives and the literature review explained, the following hypotheses were formulated:

Hypothesis 1 (H1): *The experiences lived by individuals during the quarantine have an impact on positive affects.*
Hypothesis 2 (H2): *The experiences lived by individuals during the quarantine have an impact on negative affects.*

Materials and methods

Sampling and data collection

The target population of the present study is individuals who were in Portugal during the quarantine period. In the data collection process, the non-probabilistic snowball sampling method was used, as it was considered the easiest way to operationalize the entire process due to the social isolation derived from the pandemic quarantine of COVID-19.

To create the questionnaire, we used the Google Forms. On the social network Facebook, on April 14, 2020, the link that provided access to completing the questionnaire was shared. After some sharing occurred, on June 1, 2020, data collection was completed. For ethical reasons, in the publication made on the social network Facebook, the link was accompanied by a request for participation, in which the objectives of the study were made known, as well as the guarantee of anonymity and data confidentiality, also guaranteeing that the data would only be used for statistical purposes of the present investigation and would not be disclosed to third parties.

Research instrument

The questionnaire survey used in the present investigation is of a quantitative nature and consists of three parts that address the experiences lived during the quarantine of the COVID-19 pandemic quarantine, the affects, and sociodemographic data (gender, age, educational qualifications, marital status, if have children, number of household members, and if teleworking is being carried out).

To analyze the experiences lived during the quarantine, a scale with 19 items (Table 6.1) was used, adapted from the literature review, and other scales of experiences used in the areas of marketing and tourism (Kao et al., 2008; Lee and Chang, 2012; Santos et al., 2019; Schmitt, 1999; Tsaur et al., 2007; Wu and Tseng, 2014). The items on the scale of experiences lived in the quarantine were measured using a 5-point Likert-type agreement scale (1 – *Strongly disagree* to 5 – *Strongly agree*).

To analyze affects, we use the items on the scale of well-being at work, by Paschoal and Tamayo (2008), relating to the dimensions positive and negative affects. To quantify the intensity with which individuals experience different affects, the following adjectives were used: joyful, concerned, good-natured, content, angry, depressed, bored, excited, upset, impatient, enthusiastic, anxious, happy, frustrated, annoyed, nervous, excited, tense, proud, angry, and peaceful. The scared item was also included, as from the affects literature review, in the work of Galinha et al. (2014), it presented with the most weight in the negative affects, which, given the pandemic situation, determined its inclusion in the study. Affects were assessed using a 5-point Likert-type response scale (1 – *Not a little*, 2 – *A little*, 3 – *Moderately*, 4 – *Quite*, and 5 – *Extremely*).

Table 6.1 Scale of experiences experienced during quarantine

My experience of being at home in quarantine:
E1- . . . appeals to my senses
E2- . . . it is interesting in terms of sensations
E3- . . . offers an enriching experience
E4- . . . appeals to feelings
E5- . . . gives me pleasure
E6- . . . makes me feel interested in the news from my country
E7- . . . makes me feel interested in the world news
E8- . . . stimulates my curiosity about cooking
E9- . . . appeals to my creative thinking
E10- . . . makes me think about the country's economy
E11- . . . makes me think about the future of human life
E12- . . . makes me think about my lifestyle
E13- . . . makes me want to share what I experience at home on social media
E14- . . . makes me want to take pictures for remembrance
E15- . . . makes me think about relationships
E16- . . . induces me to a feeling of identity with this way of life
E17- . . . it makes me want to visit friends/family
E18- . . . makes me want to go to the mall and buy something
E19- . . . makes me relate to the people I live with

Source: Adapted from Kao et al. (2008), Lee and Chang (2012), Santos et al. (2019), Schmitt (1999), Tsaur et al. (2007), and Wu and Tseng (2014).

Analytical methods

The collected data were analyzed using the IBM SPSS Statistics 25 and AMOS 21 software. To describe the demographic characteristics of the respondents, appropriate descriptive measures were calculated (frequency analysis, analysis of measures: mean, standard deviation, minimum, and maximum). In order to assess the reliability of the measures, Cronbach's alpha was used; to validate the constructs, exploratory factor analysis was used followed by a confirmatory factor analysis using the first-order factors. Structural equation modeling (SEM) was used to identify the structural relationships between the constructs that integrate the research model of the present study.

Results and discussion

Respondents demographic characteristics

The sample consists of 726 individuals who were in Portugal during the quarantine period, aged between 18 and 79 years, with an average age of approximately 37 years ($SD = 12.05$). Most individuals are female (55.6%) and 36.6% have children. Regarding educational qualifications, 66.3% have higher education, 32.7% have secondary or vocational education, and 1.1% have basic education. Regarding the marital status, 49.7% of individuals are married or living in a de facto relationship, 41.7% ($n = 303$) are single and 8.6% are divorced or separated or widowed, and the average number of household elements are about three ($SD = 1.17$).

Measurement model

To obtain the factors of the affect scale, an exploratory factor analysis (principal component method) was applied with Varimax rotation (factor loads with values above 0.50) and the Kaiser criterion to define the number of factors to retain (values greater than 1). The Kaiser–Meyer–Olkin (KMO) measure and Bartlett's sphericity test revealed a good sample fit (χ^2 (136) = 8226.040, $p <$ 0.001, KMO = 0.929). We obtained a factorial solution consisting of 17 items and two factors that explain 64.31% of the total variance. These factors, due to their characteristics, were called positive affect and negative affect.

Then, the confirmatory factor analysis was applied to the model resulting from the exploratory factor analysis, and after some adjustments (elimination of excited, good-natured and anxious affect items, and the addition of trajectories between residues), the adjustment indexes of the model revealed good quality of adjustment ($\chi^2 = 197.923$, $df = 69$, $\chi^2/df = 2.868$, $p < 0.001$, root mean residual [RMR] = 0.048, goodness-of-fit index [GFI] = 0.963, normed fit index [NIF] = 0.971, comparative fit index [CFI] = 0.981, root mean-squared approximation of error [RMSEA] = 0.051, probability of close fit [PCLOSE] = 0.425) according to Arbuckle (2014), Hair, Black, Babin

Table 6.2 Reliability and confirmatory analysis of the Affects Scale

Variables and items	Standardized loading (λ)	R²	CCR	AVE
Positive Affect (α = 0.911)			0.905	0.657
A1. Joyful	0.791	0.626		
A4. Content	0.829	0.687		
A8. Excited	0.818	0.669		
A11. Enthusiastic	0.740	0.548		
A13. Happy	0.870	0.757		
Negative Affect (α = 0.930)			0.927	0.585
A5. Angry	0.754	0.569		
A6. Depressed	0.789	0.623		
A9. Upset	0.784	0.615		
A10. Impatient	0.724	0.524		
A14. Frustrated	0.791	0.626		
A15. Annoyed	0.716	0.513		
A16. Nervous	0.807	0.651		
A18. Tense	0.787	0.619		
A20. Angry	0.725	0.526		

Source: Own elaboration

and Anderson (2014), and Kline (2015). Table 6.2 shows that the model's structure consists of two factors: positive affect, with five items (Joyful, Content, Excited, Enthusiastic, and Happy) and negative affect, with nine items (Angry, Depressed, Upset, Impatient, Frustrated, Annoyed, Nervous, Tense, and Angry), being in line with, for example, Ferreira et al. (2008), Galinha et al. (2014), and Gouveia et al. (2008). Standardized factorial weights range from 0.716 to 0.870 (λ ≥ 0.5), and individual reliability ranges from 0.513 to 0.757 (R^2 ≥ 0.25). Cronbach's alpha and composite reliability (CCR) values are greater than 0.90, which, according to Hair et al. (2014), it is considered a very good reliability. Average (AVE) values are greater than 0.5, which is an indicator of adequate convergent validity (Hair et al., 2014). The correlation between the positive affect and negative affect factors is negative and significant ($r = -0.292$, $p < 0.001$). As the AVE values are greater than the square of the correlation between the factors ($\gamma^2 = 0.085$) there is evidence of discriminant validity (Hair et al., 2014).

To obtain the factors of the experiences' scale lived during the quarantine, the same analyzes used for the Affects Scale were performed. Bartlett's sphericity test and the KMO index (χ^2 (45) = 3763.10, $p < 0.001$, KMO = 0.75), indicated a reasonable suitability of the sample for the exploratory factor analysis application, according to Pestana and Gageiro (2014). A factorial solution consisting of ten items and two factors was obtained, which explains 78.63% of

Table 6.3 Reliability and confirmatory analysis of the Quarantine Scale of Experiences

Variables and items	Standardized loading (λ)	R²	CCR	AVE
Sense and feel (α = 0.850)			0.853	0.661
E3 . . . offers an enriching experience	0.861	0.741		
E5 . . . give me pleasure	0.848	0.719		
E2 . . . it's interesting in terms of sensations	0.722	0.521		
Pandemic feelings (α = 0.960)			0.960	0.924
E6 . . . makes me feel interested in the news from my country	0.949	0.901		
E7 . . . makes me feel interested in the world news	0.973	0.947		
Pandemic think (α = 0.819)			0.821	0.696
E11 . . . makes me think about the future of human life	0.854	0.729		
E12 . . . makes me think about my lifestyle	0.814	0.663		
Act (α = 0.726)			0.753	0.612
E13 . . . makes me want to share what I experience at home on social media	0.626	0.392		
E14 . . . makes me want to take pictures for remembrance	0.912	0.832		

Source: Own elaboration

the total variance. These factors, due to their characteristics, were called: Sense and Feel, Pandemic Feeling, Pandemic Think, and Act.

After the elimination of item E17, which had a standardized factorial weight of less than 0.5, the confirmatory factor analysis revealed good quality adjustment indexes (χ^2 = 36.893, df = 21, χ^2/df = 1.757, $p < 0.05$, RMR = 0.029, GFI = 0.989, NFI = 0.990, CFI = 0.996, RMSEA = 0.032, PCLOSE = 0.958). Table 6.3 shows that the structure of the measurement model of the experiences lived during the quarantine is formed by four factors: Sense and Feel, with three items (E2, E3, and E5), Pandemic Feel, with two items (E6 and E7), Pandemic Think, with two items (E11 and E12), and Act, with two items (E13 and E14). Standardized factorial weights range from 0.626 to 0.973 ($\lambda \geq 0.5$), and individual reliability ranges from 0.392 to 0.947 ($R^2 \geq 0.25$). CCR values are greater than 0.70, which, according to Hair et al. (2014), it is considered a reasonable reliability. AVE values are greater than 0.5, which is an indicator of adequate convergent validity (Hair et al., 2014).

The discriminant validity of the factors was assessed by comparing the AVE with the squares of the correlations between factors. Thus, analyzing Table 6.4, it can be seen that AVE values are higher than the square of the correlation between the factors, so there is evidence of discriminant validity (Hair et al., 2014). It should also be noted that all correlation coefficients are significant at 0.1%.

Table 6.4 Analysis of the correlations between the factors of the Quarantine Scale of Experiences

	Sense and Feel	*Pandemic Feel*	*Pandemic Think*	*Act*
Sense and Feel	0.661[a]	0.133	0.255	0.213
Pandemic Feel	0.365★★★	0.924[a]	0.244	0.064
Pandemic Think	0.505★★★	0.494★★★	0.696[a]	0.115
Act	0.461★★★	0.253★★★	0.339★★★	0.612[a]

Source: Own elaboration

Note
a Diagonal elements are the AVE values. Below the diagonal are the correlation coefficients. Above the diagonal are the squared correlation coefficients. ★★★$p < 0.001$.

Table 6.5 Results of the structural model analysis

	Hypothesized path	β	B	Z	*Results*
H1	Sense and Feel → Positive Affect	0.581	0.557	10.559★★★	Supported
	Pandemic Feel → Positive Affect	0.019	0.015	0.446	Not supported
	Pandemic Think → Positive Affect	−0.121	−0.127	−2.341★	Supported
	Act → Positive Affect	0.051	0.044	1.087	Not supported
H2	Sense and Feel → Negative Affect	−0.455	−0.408	−7.708★★★	Supported
	Pandemic Feel → Negative Affect	−0.001	0.000	−0.013	Not supported
	Pandemic Think → Negative Affect	0.285	0.281	4.958★★★	Supported
	Act → Negative Affect	0.213	0.171	3.919★★★	Supported

Source: Own elaboration

★$p < 0.05$; ★★★$p < 0.001$

Structural model

After evaluating the measurement model using the confirmatory factor analysis, an analysis of structural equations was performed to test the model's validity and the formulated hypotheses. The results of the model's adjustment indexes show a good quality of adjustment ($\chi^2 = 516.182$, $df = 209$, $\chi^2/df = 2.470$, $p < 0.001$, RMR = 0.072, GFI = 0.942, NFI = 0.953, CFI = 0.971, RMSEA = 0.045, PCLOSE = 0.952) according to Arbuckle (2014), Hair et al. (2014), and Kline (2015).

Table 6.5 shows the results of the hypothesis tests that define the causal relationships between the variables. Empirical results show that Sense and Feel has a significant and positive impact on positive affect ($\beta = 0.581$, $p < 0.001$), the Pandemic Think has a significant and negative impact on positive affect ($\beta = -0.121$, $p < 0.05$), the Pandemic Feel ($\beta = 0.019$, $p > 0.05$), and the Act ($\beta = 0.051$, $p > 0.05$) do not have a significant impact on positive affect. These facts partially support Hypothesis 1.

Hypothesis 2 is also partially supported, as Sense and Feel has a significant and negative impact on negative affect ($\beta = -0.455$, $p < 0.001$), Pandemic Think has a significant and positive impact on negative affect ($\beta = 0.285$, $p < 0.001$), and the Act also has a positive impact on negative affect ($\beta = 0.213$, $p < 0.001$). Only Pandemic Feel does not have a significant impact on negative affect ($\beta = -0.001$, $p > 0.05$).

The Sense and Feel factor has a positive and significant impact on the positive affect factor and a negative impact on the negative affect factor, which is found in alignment with the thinking of Van Horn et al. (2004), which states that the affects can be characterized by the frequency of feelings and emotions arising from situations that result from favorable or unfavorable experiences. The Pandemic Think factor has a negative impact on positive affect and a positive impact on negative affect, and the Act factor only has a positive impact on negative affect. This result can be explained due to the change in lifestyles and behaviors due to the quarantine situation, which may have psychological impacts on individuals (Desclaux et al., 2017).

Conclusions

The aim of this article was to study the impact of experiences on affects during the COVID-19 pandemic quarantine. Through the use of a questionnaire survey, a sample of 726 individuals who were in Portugal during the quarantine and confinement period was analyzed.

The structure of the affects scale consists of two factors: positive affect and negative affect. The structure of the scale of experiences lived during the quarantine is formed by four factors: Sense and Feel, Pandemic Feel, Pandemic Think, and Act. Both scales showed adequate convergent, discriminant validity, and internal consistency.

The results show that the experiences lived during quarantine, in general, have an impact on affects. The senses and sensations have a positive influence on positive affects and a negative influence on negative affects, depending on whether the situation is favorable or unfavorable. Thinking about the pandemic negatively influences positive affect and positively influences negative affect; actions only positively influence negative affect.

It is expected that the present study will help students, teachers, and researchers to better understand the experiences and affects experienced in a situation of quarantine and confinement. The results found to become useful for health professionals to define appropriate strategies to improve the way individuals experience the experiences and affects and consequently improve the well-being and health of individuals.

For individuals who were to perform telework from their homes, the importance of holding meetings between coworkers is emphasized, where knowledge and work experiences are shared in order to maintain the group's socialization, and the sense of unity and belonging to the company. Of course, coworkers' birthday celebrations can complement these meetings and thus reduce the frequency and intensity of negative affective experiences (Couto and Paschoal, 2017). It would be very important for the company to provide its employees with an online support office with professionals who interact with workers in times of more stress and anxiety, thus preventing the occurrence of illnesses.

For individuals who were on layoff, it will be very important to create online training to occupy their time and, at the same time, increase knowledge in professional areas. For individuals with a tendency to depressive illnesses, we consider it important to create support lines with appropriate health professionals to try to keep, even at a distance, individuals under surveillance.

In this study, younger populations (under the age of 18 years) were not studied. However, support for this population cannot be forgotten, as children and young people today will be adults of the near future. This could be a future study, that is, to study the impact of experiences on affects in younger populations. During quarantine, the younger populations kept busy, attending classes remotely and also synchronously with their teachers. It is recommended that schools schedule support from professionals, for example, private conversations where children or young people can expose their doubts and concerns, and also the realization of online games that work synchronously, to maintain social contact, even if virtual.

References

Agapito, D. L., Mendes, J. C., Valle, P. S. and Almeida, H. (2014) 'Um contributo do marketing sensorial para o marketing da experiência turística rural', *PASOS Revista de Turismo y Patrimonio Cultural*, 12(3): 611–621.

Arbuckle, J. L. (2014) *IBM® Amos TM 23 user's guide*. Chicago: Amos Development Corporation.

Cava, M. A., Fay, K. E, Beanlands, H. J., McCay, E. A. and Wignall, R. (2005) 'The experience of quarantine for individuals affected by SARS in Toronto', *Public Health Nursing*, 22: 398–406.

Cohen, J. B., Pham, M. T. and Andrade, E. B. (2008) 'The nature and role of affect in consumer behavior', In C. P. Haugtvedt, P. Herr and F. Kardes (Eds.), *Handbook of consumer psychology* (pp. 297–348). Mahwah, NJ: Lawrence Erlbaum.

Corrêa, S. B. and Gouvêa, V. M. (2019) 'Causas e experiências: Percursos para gerar impactos e transformações', *Mídia e Cultura Contemporânea: Série Linguagem*, 4.

Couto, P. R. and Paschoal, T. (2017) 'Relação entre ações de qualidade de vida no trabalho e bem-estar laboral', *Psicologia Argumento*, 30(70): 585–593.

Desclaux, A., Badji, D., Ndione, A. G. and Sow, K. (2017) 'Accepted monitoring or endured quarantine? Ebola contacts' perceptions in Senegal', *Social Science & Medicine*, 178: 38–45.

Diener, E. (2000) 'Subjective well-being: The science of happiness, and a proposal for national index', *American Psychologist*, 55: 34–43.

Diener, E. and Larsen, R. J. (1984) 'Temporal stability and cross-situational consistency of affective, behavioral, and cognitive responses', *Journal of Personality and Social Psychology*, 47(4): 871–883.

Diener, E., Lucas, R. and Oishi, S. (2005) 'Subjective well-being – The science of happiness and life satisfaction', In C. R. Snyder and S. J. Lopez (Eds.), *Handbook of positive psychology* (pp. 63–73). Oxford: Oxford University Press.

Diener, E., Pressman, S. D., Hunter, J. and Delgadillo-Chase, D. (2017) 'If, why, and when subjective well-being influences health, and future needed research', *Applied Psychology: Health and Well-Being*, 9: 133–167.

Diener, E. and Ryan, K. (2009) 'Subjective well-being: A general overview', *South African Journal of Psychology*, 39(4): 391–406.

Esteves, L. P. and Ribeiro, S. (2016) 'A importância dos vínculos afetivos e da interação familiar para a formação e aprendizagem escolar das crianças', *Revista Psicologia, Diversidade e Saúde*, 5(2): 206–214.

Ferraz, R. B., Tavares, H. and Zilberman, M. L., (2007) 'Felicidade: uma revisão', *Archives of Clinical Psychiatry*, 34(5): 234–242.

Ferreira, M. C., Correa, A. P., Fernandes, H. A. and Almeida, S. P. (2008) 'Desenvolvimento e validação de uma escala de afetos no trabalho (ESAFE)', *Avaliação Psicológica*, 7(2): 143–150.

Galinha, I. C., Pereira, C. R. and Esteves, F. (2014) 'Versão reduzida da escala portuguesa de afeto positivo e negativo-PANAS-VRP: Análise fatorial confirmatória e invariância temporal', *Psicologia*, 28(1): 50–62.

Gouveia, V. V., Fonsêca, P. N. D., Lins, S. L. B., Lima, A. V. D. and Gouveia, R. S. (2008) 'Escala de bem-estar afetivo no trabalho (JAWS): evidências de validade fatorial e consistência interna', *Psicologia: Reflexão e Crítica*, 21(3): 464–473.

Gray, E. K. and Watson, D. (2007) 'Assessing positive and negative affect via self-report', *Handbook of Emotion Elicitation and Assessment*: 171–183.

Grundey, D. (2008) 'Experiential marketing vs. traditional marketing: Creating rational and emotional liaisons with consumers', *The Romanian Economic Journal*, 29(3): 133–151.

Hair, J. F., Black, W. C., Babin, B. J. and Anderson, R. E. (2014) *Multivariate data analysis*, 7th ed. Edinburgh: Pearson.

Harris, C., Daniels, K. and Briner, R. (2003) 'A daily diary study of goals and affective well-being at work', *Journal of Occupational and Organizational Psychology*, 73: 401–410.

Hirschle, A. L. T., Gondim, S. M. G., Alberton, G. D. and Ferreira, A. S. M. (2019) 'Estresse e bem-estar no trabalho: o papel moderador da regulação emocional', *Revista Psicologia: Organizações e Trabalho*, 19(1): 532–540.

Huang, C., Wang, Y., Li, X., Ren, L., Zhao, J., Hu, Y. and Cheng, Z. (2020) 'Clinical features of patients infected with 2019 novel coronavirus in Wuhan, China', *The Lancet*, 395(10223): 497–506.

Ivtzan, I., Lomas, T., Hefferon, K. and Worth, P. (2015) *Second wave positive psychology embracing the dark side of life*. London: Routledge.

Kao, Y. F., Huang, L. S. and Wu, C. H. (2008) 'Effects of theatrical elements on experiential quality and loyalty intentions for theme parks', *Asia Pacific Journal of Tourism Research*, 13(2): 163–174.

Kesebir, P. and Diener, E. (2008) 'In pursuit of happiness: Empirical answers to philosophical questions', *Perspectives on Psychological Science*, 3: 117–125.

Keyes, C., Shmotkin, D. and Ryff, C. (2002) 'Optimizing well-being: The empirical encounter of two traditions', *Journal of Personality and Social Psychology*, 82(6): 1007–1022.

Kline, R. B. (2015) *Principles and practice of structural equation modeling*, 4th ed. New York: Guilford Press.

La Placa, V., McNaught, A. and Knight, A. (2013) 'Discourse on wellbeing in research and practice', *International Journal of Wellbeing*, 3(1): 116–125.

Lee, T. H. and Chang, Y. S. (2012) 'The influence of experiential marketing and activity involvement on the loyalty intentions of wine tourists in Taiwan', *Leisure Studies*, 31(1): 103–121.

Nakano, T. D. C., Machado, W. D. L. and Abreu, I. C. C. D. (2019) 'Relaciones entre estilos de pensar y crear, bienestar, salud percibida y estrés en la vejez', *Psico-USF*, 24(3): 555–568.

Noronha, A. P. P., Delforno, M. P. and Pinto, L. P. (2014) 'Afetos positivos e negativos em professores de diferentes níveis de ensino', *Psicologia Escolar e Educacional*, 18(2): 211–218.

Paschoal, T. and Tamayo, A. (2008) 'Construção e validação da escala de bem-estar no trabalho', *Avaliação Psicológica*, 7(1): 11–22.

Pestana, M. H. and Gageiro, J. N. (2014) *Análise de dados em Ciências Sociais – A complementaridade do SPSS*, 6th ed. Lisboa: Sílabo.

Same, S. and Larimo, J. (2012) 'Marketing theory: Experience marketing and experiential marketing', *7th International Scientific Conference Business and Management 2012* (10–11 May), pp. 10–11. LITHUANIA Vilnius Gediminas Technical University, Vilnis.

Santos, M. C., Gibim, Q. G. M. T. and Wechsler, S. M. (2020) 'Relação entre criatividade e otimismo', *Revista Ibero-Americana de Criatividade e Inovação-RECRIAI*, 1(1): 1.

Santos, V., Santos, E., Caldeira, A., Oliveira, S. and Miguel, I. (2019) 'The experience in the visits to Tejo Region's Wine Tourism Units', *Proceedings of the 2nd International Conference on Tourism Research 2019* (ICTR19, 14–15 March), pp. 274–281, University Portucalense, Porto, Portugal.

Satuf, C., Monteiro, S., Pereira, H., Esgalhado, G., Afonso, R. M. and Loureiro, M. (2018) 'The protective effect of job satisfaction in health, happiness, well-being and self-esteem', *International Journal of Occupational Safety and Ergonomics*, 24(2): 181–189.

Scherer, K. R. (2005) 'What are emotions? And how can they be measured?', *Social Science Information*, 44(4): 695–729.

Schmitt, B. (1999) 'Experiential marketing', *Journal of Marketing Management*, 15(1–3): 53–67.

Seligman, M. and Csikszentmihalyi, M. (2000) 'Positive psychology: An introduction', *American Psycologist*, 55(1): 5–14.

Soraggi, F. and Paschoal, T. (2011) 'Relação entre bem-estar no trabalho, valores pessoais e oportunidades de alcance de valores pessoais no trabalho', *Estudos e Pesquisas em Psicologia*, 11(2): 614–632.

Tooby, J. and Cosmides, L. (2008) 'The evolutionary psychology of the emotions and their relationship to internal regulatory variables', In M. Lewis, J. M. Haviland-Jones and L. F. Barrett (Eds.), *Handbook of emotions*, 3rd ed. (pp. 114–137). New York, NY: The Guilford Press.

Tsaur, S. H., Chiu, Y. T. and Wang, C. H. (2007) 'The visitors behavioral consequences of experiential marketing: An empirical study on Taipei Zoo', *Journal of Travel & Tourism Marketing*, 21(1): 47–64.

Van Horn, J., Taris, T., Schaufeli, W. and Scheurs, P. (2004) 'The structure of occupational well-being: A study among Dutch teachers', *Journal of Occupational and Organizational Psychology*, 77: 365–375.

Wallon, H. (1979) *Origens do pensamento na criança*. São Paulo: Manole.

Wesarat, P. O., Sharif, M. Y. and Majid, A. H. A. (2015) 'A conceptual framework of happiness at the workplace', *Asian Social Science*, 11(2): 78–88.

Wong, S. S. and Lim, T. (2009) 'Hope versus optimism in Singaporean adolescents: Contributions to depression and life satisfaction', *Personality and Individual Differences*, 46: 648–652.

World Health Organization and World Organisation for Animal Health (2011) *Report of the WHO Informal Working Group on Cystic and Alveolar Echinococcosis Surveillance, Prevention and Control, with the Participation of the Food and Agriculture Organization of the United Nations and the World Organisation for Animal Health*. Geneva: World Health Organization.

Worldometers (2020) *Covid-19 coronavirus pandemic*, www.worldometers.info/coronavirus/, last visited 18th July 2020.

Wu, M.-Y. and Tseng, L.-H. (2014) 'Customer satisfaction and loyalty in an online shop: An experiential marketing perspective', *International Journal of Business and Management*, 10(1): 104.

Zanon, C., Bastianello, M. R., Pacico, J. C. and Hutz, C. S. (2013) 'Desenvolvimento e validação de uma escala de afetos positivos e negativos', *Psico-USF*, 18(2): 193–201.

7 The perception of middle managers on the organizational environment for the promotion of entrepreneurship and innovation activities in organizations

Aquilino Felizardo, Eulália Santos, Andrea Sousa, and Vanessa Ratten

Introduction

According to Kuratko, Hornsby and Bishop (2005), there is an important relationship between the organizational environment, the behavior of entrepreneurial managers, and the organizational entrepreneurship actions implementation. Among the several factors that some studies suggest are important to organizational entrepreneurship promotion, Hornsby, Kuratko and Zahra (2002) emphasize the vital role played by middle-level managers in creating an environment that stimulates innovation and entrepreneurship.

This organizational entrepreneurial environment, being a form of expression of entrepreneurial within the organization (Hornsby et al., 2002), is also called as *intrapreneurship* (Goldsby, Kuratko, Hornsby, Houghton and Neck, 2006). This designation also applies to organizations with entrepreneurial attitudes (Covin and Slevin, 1991) whose activities benefit and revitalize organizational performance (Antoncic and Hisrich, 2001). But to better understand intrapreneurship, it is necessary to place it in the concept of 'Entrepreneurship Organization' as an important activity for the company's vitality (Dess, Ireland, Zahra, Floyd, Janney and Lane, 2003). According to the analysis' level of organizational entrepreneurship mentioned above, several authors have used the concept of entrepreneurial orientation to characterize the companies that adopt this type of behavior.

In this perspective, the entrepreneurial orientation refers to the strategic development practices used to identify and promote an organizational enterprise, translated in the strategic processes (Lumpkin and Dess, 1996, 2001) and the organizational culture of the company (Covin, Green and Slevin, 2006). Therefore, entrepreneurial organization is also a type of organizational behavior, in which behaviors, as a central and essential element in the entrepreneurship process are what give meaning to the entrepreneurial process, unlike attributes (Covin and Slevin, 1991).

Regarding the middle-level managers' role, the research suggests that they are the pivot where organizational knowledge flows (Floyd and Wooldridge, 1992). Their positioning in the leadership structure, placed between top managers and first-line managers, allows them to influence and shape entrepreneurial strategies in the organizations. By promoting innovative activities in both processes and products/services, they enable not only to stimulate interest in organizational entrepreneurship but also to create the conditions to influence the commitment of their subordinates (Hornsby et al., 2002).

Besides that, understanding the middle-level managers' perception of the internal organizational environment is crucial to start and sustain any entrepreneurial process (Hornsby et al., 2002). The authors also pointed out that some researchers have sought to identify certain variables that affect the scope of entrepreneurship by an organization, including internal factors such as incentives and control, culture, structure, and management support.

The emphasis given in the literature of middle-level management is consistent with the increasing recognition of the key role that these managers play in promoting organizational entrepreneurship (Floyd and Wooldridge, 1992; Hornsby et al., 2002). Despite the importance recognized by the research on entrepreneurial organizations and the role of middle-level managers in stimulating and sustaining these organizations, Goldsby et al. (2006) reported the presence of a scarce development of the literature regarding the cognitive processes of middle-level managers involved in entrepreneurial activities.

In this sense, we placed as a research question for our empirical study: *What is the perception of middle-managers on the internal conditions that influence their participation in the promotion of entrepreneurship activities in their organizations.*

Based on the study of Hornsby et al. (2002), in which the authors developed an instrument (corporate entrepreneurship assessment instrument [CEAI]) to identify empirically the internal conditions that influence the participation of the middle-level management in the organizational entrepreneurship's activities, we applied a questionnaire survey to managers of middle-level in nonfinancial organizations with activity in Portugal. The objective was to assess the perception of these on the internal factors that may be influencing or conditioning their behavior as an entrepreneur.

Given the overwhelming majority of Portuguese organizations are small, their organizational structures change the concept of middle-level managers predominant in the literature. For this reason, we opted for the concept advocated by Floyd and Wooldridge (1992) that define middle-level managers as those who perform management functions (albeit informally) in the functional departments that are part of their structure, regardless of their organizational model and as long as they report to a top hierarchy considered top management.

Intrapreneurship

The intrapreneurship can be seen as a means by which companies can develop the ability of their employees to innovate. As an important element in organizational and economic development, Antoncic and Hisrich (2001) define intrapreneurship as 'entrepreneurship within organizations.'

In the study that Zahra (1991) carried out, the author verified that intrapreneurship leads to the product, the process of innovation, and the development of the market.

The conceptions about intrapreneurship developed by Antoncic and Hisrich (2001) and Foba and De Villiers (2007), classified it into four dimensions:

- adventure in new business – seeking and entering new business within the existing organization, redefining its products/services, and developing new markets;
- innovation – creation of new products, services, and technologies;
- self-renewal – strategy reformulation, reorganization, and organizational change;
- proactivity – top management orientation in search of greater competitiveness.

Beyond these four dimensions, Foba and De Villiers (2007) added five secondary features that can be found, if not most in all intrapreneurs: strategy, innovation, autonomy, risk-taking, and teamwork.

In this regard, Sarkar (2014) considers that 'intrapreneurs are entrepreneurs who operate successfully in an established organization or in partnership with other entrepreneurs who possess the attributes and capacities that they do not have' (p. 36).

Entrepreneurship organization

Covin and Slevin (1991) describe entrepreneurship as the dimension of a company's strategic posture, represented by a propensity to assume risks, a tendency to act competitively aggressive, a proactive attitude, and a dependency for product innovation. In the same vein, Lumpkin and Dess (1996) and Kuratko et al. (2005) argue that any organization, which engages in a combination of autonomy, innovation, risk-taking, proactivity, and competitive aggressiveness is entrepreneurial.

On the other hand, Zahra (1991) states that one can also consider 'organizational entrepreneurship' as formal or informal activities, aimed at creating new business in existing organizations through product and process innovation and market development. These activities can be located at the organizational, divisional, functional, or project level (Kuratko et al., 2005).

In this perspective, an entrepreneurial organization is concerned; therefore, with the various forms of novelty and its impact on performance, growth, and even organizational survival, because it is through organizational entrepreneurship that organizations develop knowledge and use it as a source of innovations to overcome competition (Dess et al., 2003).

However, the essence of the activity of an entrepreneurial organization is still not clear enough (Kuratko et al., 2005), since it depends on internal and external factors of the context where the organization is inserted (Barringer and Bluedorn, 1999). This environment in which most organizations face today is characterized by its dynamism which, due to uncertainties, not only poses threats but also reveals opportunities (Hitt, Ireland, Sirmon and Trahms, 2011).

But as managers individually acquire knowledge and skills through their entrepreneurial behavior, organizations can also learn and develop skills by implementing organizational entrepreneurship strategies (Ireland, Covin and Kuratko, 2009). However, leveraging the employees' knowledge and experience to innovate and stay ahead of the competition is still underutilized by companies (Sarkar, 2014).

Barringer and Bluedorn (1999) study results on the relationship between entrepreneurial organization and strategic management suggest that the intensity of entrepreneurship in the organization is influenced by the nature of the practices of its strategic management. Given its breadth, the concept of entrepreneurial organization tends to be studied at different levels within the organization and under different perspectives of analysis (Kuratko et al., 2005). In this sense, Lumpkin and Dess (1996) refer to entrepreneurial organization as an entrepreneurial orientation, Brown, Davidsson and Wiklund (2001) as entrepreneurial management, and Zahra (1993) as organizational behavior.

In this context, Ireland et al. (2009) propose a business organization strategy's model that includes, as one of its components, elements of entrepreneurial orientations that are reflected in entrepreneurial behavior, such as: (1) a strategic entrepreneurial vision of top management; (2) an organizational architecture that stimulates entrepreneurial processes and behaviors; and (3) generic forms of the entrepreneurial process.

Entrepreneurship orientation

Lumpkin and Dess (1996, 2001) have drawn a distinction between the concepts of entrepreneurial orientation and entrepreneurship. According to the authors, while entrepreneurial orientation represents processes, entrepreneurship refers to the content of decisions. Their analysis can be better understood through the key dimensions that the authors characterize as business orientations, which are:

(1) a propensity for autonomy – which refers to independent, individual, or group action in realizing an idea or vision;
(2) a willingness to innovate – reflected by the organization's ability to engage and to develop new ideas that culminate in new products and services;
(3) a willingness to take risks – make resources available to explore opportunities and to launch new projects, despite the uncertainty of results;

(4) a tendency for competitive aggressiveness – a propensity in which an organization directly and intensely challenges its competitors with a view to entering new markets or improving its position; and

(5) a proactiveness to market opportunities – namely to initiate other activities.

However, the authors point out that these dimensions may be independent depending on the organizational context and the external environment in which they are inserted.

With another contribution in this area of study, Antoncic and Hisrich (2001) relate the 'innovation' dimension with technological leadership, supported by the R&D processes in the development of new products, services, and processes. In this sense, a strategic entrepreneurial vision represents a commitment to innovation, business processes, and behaviors, expressed as the organization's modus operandi (Ireland et al., 2009).

In this perspective, an entrepreneurial orientation can be seen as a conducting wire of new business within organizations (Dess et al., 2003) and as a process of organizational renewal (Hornsby et al., 2002). However, the entrepreneurial orientation approach suggests that it is in the top managers' behavior that organizational entrepreneurship can be manifested (Covin et al., 2006).

Organizational behavior

Schein (1992) defines 'organizational culture' as a set of basic assumptions and beliefs shared by members of a group or an organization, involving a vision, the potential to shape behavior, reinforce common beliefs, and encourage members to apply their efforts to achieve organizational goals.

Kuratko et al. (2005) argue that entrepreneurial behavior is increasingly recognized as an advocate for social change and facilitator of innovation within organizations. To reinforce this idea, Sarkar (2014) argues that 'An entrepreneurial culture allows the flourishing of entrepreneurship, [and create] a virtuous circle where they can appear more entrepreneurs' (p. 78), since as the managers' entrepreneurial behavior increases, the satisfaction of their subordinates also increases (Kuratko et al., 2005).

In this perspective that organizational behavior leads to individual and organizational results, Ireland et al. (2009) propose that entrepreneurial behavior can be observed at the level of the members of the organization and not at the level of top management, concerned with the organization's vision. However, the perspective of entrepreneurial orientation suggests that it is in top management behavior that organizational entrepreneurship manifests itself (Covin et al., 2006). In this sense, we would say that an entrepreneurial organization refers not only to entrepreneurship in organizations but also to a type of organizational behavior.

In this regard, Barringer and Bluedorn (1999) point out that entrepreneurial attitudes and behaviors are necessary for organizations to flourish in competitive environments, so that different types of behavior can be carried out by only one person, such as small organizations, but also by several people, in the case of medium or large companies or in projects (Hayton and Kelley, 2006).

Middle-level managers

A manager is someone who coordinates and oversees the work of others to achieve organizational goals. More than achieving their own fulfillment, their key role is to help others to perform better their duties, so that the top-, middle-level, and first-line managers have different responsibilities for each organizational entrepreneurship subprocess (Floyd and Wooldridge, 1992; Floyd and Lane, 2000).

Although managers at the various levels have an important strategic role for the organization success, research on entrepreneurial organization often highlights the importance of the middle-level managers' actions to create new businesses or even to reconfigure the existing ones (Floyd and Lane, 2000, Kuratko et al., 2005). This importance is manifested, on the one hand by the need for middle-level managers to behave in an entrepreneurial way and, on the other hand, in the requirement to support and to encourage other employees to adopt the same behavior, since those who do not have an entrepreneurial posture have a negative impact on innovation processes (Goldsby et al., 2006).

In addition, the role of mid-level managers as agents of change and innovation promoters, facilitated by their central position in the organization, positions them as a crucial element in business strategy (Floyd and Lane, 2000), once they tend to facilitate the flow of information to support the development and implementation of projects (Goldsby et al., 2006).

Some studies have demonstrated the relevance of the role played by middle-level managers in creating an environment that encourages innovation and entrepreneurship and in search for new ideas combining knowledge (Hornsby, Kuratko, Shepherd and Bott, 2009), whose influence goes beyond the strategies implementation (Floyd and Wooldridge, 1992).

By acting as a bridge between those at the top level and those at the operational or front-line level, middle-level managers assume actions that influence both directions of the hierarchy. In this perspective, Floyd and Wooldridge (1992) define intermediate management as the coordination between the activities of an organizational unit and the activities of vertically linked groups.

The position that these managers take in the organizations allows them to gather, to absorb, and to explore new ideas combining knowledge inside or outside the organization, giving way to its development. In this process, they become responsible for communicating the potential of these ideas to other organization members, seeking for support and resources to their implementation (Hornsby et al., 2009).

Internal factors

An internal environment conducive to intrapreneurship seems to be related to organizational processes that converge on five factors: (1) appropriate use of rewards; (2) support from top management; (3) availability of resources; (4) organizational support structure; and (5) risk-taking and tolerance for failure (Hornsby et al., 2002; Marvel, Griffin, Hebda and Vojak, 2007; Alpkan, Bulut, Gunday, Ulusoy and Kilic, 2010).

The *appropriate use of rewards* consists of individually considering the objectives and their evaluation based on the results, in order to increase the willingness of an individual to assume the risks associated with the activity (Marvel et al., 2007). In this sense, the individual must realize that the organization has a reward system based on entrepreneurship and success (Hornsby et al., 2002, 2009).

The *top management support* refers to the willingness of these managers to facilitate and promote entrepreneurial activities in organizations (Kuratko et al., 2005). This support can configure in several ways, such as defending new ideas, providing the necessary resources or knowledge, defending innovative ideas, and establishing entrepreneurial activities within the company (Marvel et al., 2007; Hornsby et al., 2009), so the success of intrapreneurship depends largely on leadership (Sarkar, 2014). Hence the importance of top managers working, on the one hand, to create an organizational architecture in order that entrepreneurship initiatives are developed without their direct involvement (Ireland et al., 2009) and, on the other hand, to intervene in problems-solving and conflicts resolution during the cycle of ideas: generation, development, and implementation (Alpkan et al., 2010).

But employees need to perceive the existence of *resources available* for innovation processes, such as time, a necessary condition for organizational entrepreneurship (Marvel et al., 2007). This availability of free time is a critical factor for daily routines and intrapreneurial ideas and activities, that is, time is needed to imagine, observe, experiment, and develop new ideas (Alpkan et al., 2010).

An *organizational structure* to support organizational entrepreneurial provides administrative mechanisms that allow the ideas are evaluated, selected, and implemented (Marvel et al., 2007). An organizational structure that affords an intrapreneurship climate should particularly involve the autonomy and flexibility (Alpkan et al., 2010), so that employees can make decisions about their work (Hornsby et al., 2002) and implement them in order to realize their ideas (Lumpkin and Dess, 1996, Alpkan et al., 2010).

Finally, managers and employees must be willing not only to *take risks* but also to be tolerant with the failures (Marvel et al., 2007). The willingness of the intrapreneur to take risks, as well as the risk assumed by the top manager by allowing and encouraging the employee to be more innovative, requires a more tolerant understanding of failure, especially in more turbulent markets (Hornsby et al., 2002; Alpkan et al., 2010). The top managers' attitudes and behaviors are important to create support for the internal environment, whereby intrapreneurs need to realize that they will not be punished, and there will be tolerance for the failures that are due from actions considered in good faith (Lumpkin and Dess, 1996; Alpkan et al., 2010).

Hornsby, Kuratko, and Zahra study

The study that underlies the present empirical research of the authors Hornsby et al. (2002), aimed to understand middle-level management perceptions about the internal corporate environment. In that study, the authors developed an organizational entrepreneurship assessment tool (CEAI).

The instrument was validated by the factorial analysis, which confirmed the existence of five factors that influence the middle-level managers' behavior to promote entrepreneurship activities in their organizations: (1) management support for corporate entrepreneurship; (2) work discretion; (3) rewards/reinforcement; (4) time availability; and (5) organizational boundaries.

The results of the study also indicated that the evaluation tool developed can be a useful instrument for diagnosing a company's environment about organizational entrepreneurship in order: (1) to identify areas where intermediate-level managers can make a significant difference; (2) to develop strategies that can stimulate and support entrepreneurship in the organization; and (3) to help defining the area of middle-level managers influence, by providing them with greater involvement in strengthening entrepreneurial activities.

Methodology

The data collection instrument selected to inquire the middle-level managers was a closed response questionnaire constituted by three parts. The first (group A) and third (group C) parts collect the data to characterize the respondents and organizations where they perform their function. The second part (group B), consisting of 43 items distributed by the five factors (Table 7.1) was elaborated according to the evaluation instrument (CEAI) developed and validated by Hornsby et al. (2002). For each of the 43 items, participants responded according to a Likert-type five-point scale (1 – *strongly disagree*, 2 – *disagree*, 3 – *partially agree*, 4 – *agree*, and 5 – *totally agree*). The third part aims to characterize the organizations where managers carry out their roles (activity area, number of departments, number of employees, sales volume, and geographical location of the organization).

Table 7.1 Comparison of the internal consistency analysis between the two studies

Dimensions	No. of items	Cronbach's alphas Hornsby et al. (2002)	Cronbach's alphas in the present study
Management support for corporate entrepreneurship	17	0.89	0.96
Work discretion	10	0.87	0.90
Rewards/reinforcement	5	0.75	0.91
Time availability	6	0.77	0.81
Organizational boundaries	5	0.64	0.82

The CEAI was translated from English into Portuguese language by a translator and then reviewed by a Portuguese language specialist. A pretest was carried out with the collaboration of seven middle-level managers to assess the clarity of the questions that, after being evaluated and taken into account, we proceed to minor semantic adjustments.

The survey was carried out on the LimeSurvey digital platform, through which the data were collected. This tool enables a faster collection process and guarantees the anonymous and confidential nature of the responses.

From an invitation sent to 624 organizations from various sectors of nonfinancial business activity in Portugal requesting their participation, we obtained 73 responses. Sixty-six were validated, corresponding to a response rate of 10.6%.

The seven responses not considered were incomplete because they did not answer the questions of group B.

The collected data were subjected to a statistical treatment with the use of version 23.0 of the software IBM SPSS Statistics. The internal consistency of the instrument was verified by calculating the values of the Cronbach alphas of the five dimensions of the instrument developed by Hornsby et al. (2002). To perform the characterization of managers and organizations, and the study of managers' perceptions about the internal organizational environment, we used descriptive statistics and, to test the hypotheses, we used linear regression analysis and statistical inference techniques: correlation coefficient of Pearson and Spearman, Kruskal–Wallis test, and Student's *t* test for comparison of independent samples.

The five factors obtained by Hornsby et al. (2002) explain 43.3% of the variance. The internal consistency values obtained in the present study and the study by Hornsby et al. (2002) are shown in Table 7.1. The results show that the instrument has a good internal consistency (Pestana and Gageiro, 2014). In the present study, the Cronbach's alpha values were higher than those obtained by Hornsby et al. (2002).

Results and discussion

Characterization of respondents and organizations

Of the 66 managers who answered the questionnaire, 68.2% ($n = 45$) were male and 31.8% ($n = 21$) were female. Among the functions they carry out in the organizations, stand out the direction of marketing/commercial/sales management (27.3%, $n = 18$), general management (27.3%, $n = 18$) and human resources management (13.6%, $n = 9$). The remaining functions are distributed equitably by other organizational departments.

Most managers (62.1%, $n = 41$) have been collaborating with the organization for more than 5 years. Regarding the time they hold the position, 51.5% ($n = 34$) of managers have held the position for more than 5 years and are responsible for 1–44 employees, with an average of approximately 13 collaborators ($SD = 11.84$).

Regarding the characterization of the organizations that managers belong, these are distributed equally by areas of industry activity (50.0%, *n* = 33) and trade/services (50.0%, *n* = 33). As for the organizational structure, the organizations have 1–8 departments that coordinate between 2 and 1620 employees, with a sales volume ranging between 40,000 and 88 million euros, thus covering micro (19.7%, *n* = 13), small (39.4%, *n* = 26), medium (27.3%, *n* = 18), and large organizations (13.6%, *n* = 9), which according to their location cover the different areas of Portugal.

Perceptions of middle managers on the internal organizational environment

In general, middle-level managers have reasonable levels of perception about organization's internal environment (*M* = 3.32, *SD* = 0.62). Through the analysis of Figure 7.1, we can observe that the dimension *work discretion* is the one that presents a higher average perception (*M* = 3.73, *SD* = 0.70), and the dimension *management support for corporate entrepreneurship* is the one that presents lower average perception levels (*M* = 3.10, *SD* = 0.91). It should be noted that in the study of Hornsby et al. (2002) for middle-level managers it was also the work discretion dimension that presents higher mean values.

It is also highlighted that the three items with the highest average levels of agreement that are included in the dimension *work discretion* are: 'This organization provides freedom to use my own judgment' (*M* = 4.18, *SD* = 0.84); 'I have

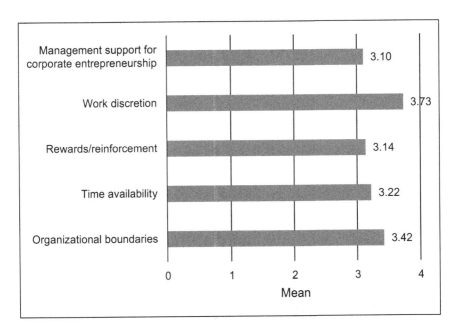

Figure 7.1 Middle managers' perception results about the internal organizational environment

the freedom to decide what I do on my job' (M = 4.09; SD = 0.74); and 'It is basically my own responsibility to decide how my job gets done' (M = 4.05, SD = 0.77). However, the item with lower mean level of agreement is 'Harsh criticism and punishment result from mistakes made on the job' (M = 2.41, SD = 0.84). In relation to the other two items with lower average levels of agreement belong to the dimension *management support for corporate entrepreneurship* are: 'Money is often available to get new ideas off the ground' (M = 2.45, SD = 1.13) and 'Promotion usually follows the development of new and innovative ideas' (M = 2.45, SD = 1.13).

As we can see from Table 7.2, the dimension *time availability* only shows a statistically significant correlation with the *rewards/reinforcement* dimension, which is negative and weak (r = −0.26). These results show that managers perceive that increasing the availability of time diminishes the rewards. It is also verified that there are positive and significant correlations between the remaining dimensions, with the highest correlation occurring between the dimensions *rewards/reinforcement* and *management support for corporate entrepreneurship* (r = 0.85), and the weaker correlation occurs between the dimensions *organizational boundaries* and *time availability*.

To ascertain if the willingness of top managers to facilitate and promote entrepreneurial activities positively influences *work discretion, reward/reinforcement,* and *organizational boundaries*, we applied a linear regression analysis.

Thus, it can be stated that 56.1% of total variability *work discretion* is explained by the willingness of top managers to facilitate and promote entrepreneurial activities. The model proved to be adjusted and significant (F(1, 64) = 81.918, p = 0.000 < 0.01), so it can be inferred that this is adequate and there is a linear dependence between the dimensions *management support for corporate entrepreneurship* and *work discretion*. The top managers' willingness to facilitate and to promote entrepreneurial activity influences significantly (t(65) = 9.051, p = 0.000 < 0.01) *work discretion* and there is a positive variation (β = 0.749).

Table 7.2 Results of Pearson's correlation between the dimensions of the internal organizational environment perception

	Management support for corporate entrepreneurship	Work discretion	Rewards/ reinforcement	Time availability
Work discretion	0.75**			
Rewards/ reinforcement	0.85**	0.58**		
Time availability	−0.09	0.03	−0.26*	
Organizational boundaries	0.55**	0.78**	0.34**	0.32**

**p < 0.01; *p < 0.05

We can also note that 73% of the total variability of *reward/reinforcement* is explained by the desire on the part of senior management to facilitate and promote entrepreneurial activities. Through analysis of variance (ANOVA) ($F(1, 64) = 172.791$, $p = 0.000 < 0.01$) it can be inferred that this model is adequate, there being a linear dependence between the dimensions *management support for corporate entrepreneurship* and *reward/reinforcement*. The top managers' willingness to facilitate and to promote entrepreneurial activity influences statistically ($t(65) = 13.145$, $p = 0.000 < 0.01$) and positively ($\beta = 0.854$) the reward systems.

Finally, only 30.5% of the total variability of organizational boundaries is explained by the willingness of top managers to facilitate and promote entrepreneurial activities. The model proved to be adjusted and significant ($F(1, 64) = 28.122$, $p = 0.000 < 0.01$), so it can be inferred that there is a linear dependence between dimensions *management support for corporate entrepreneurship* and *organizational boundaries*. The top managers' willingness to facilitate and to promote entrepreneurial activities influences statistically ($t(65) = 5.303$, $p = 0.000 < 0.01$) and positively ($\beta = 0.553$) the organizational boundaries. In this way, it can be inferred that the willingness of top managers to facilitate and to promote entrepreneurial activities positively influences *work discretion, reward/reinforcement,* and *organizational boundaries*.

Through the application of the Spearman correlation, we verified that the time in the organization ($\rho = -0.162$; $p = 0.193 > 0.05$) and the time in the position ($\rho = -0.069$; $p = 0.581 > 0.05$) do not present statistically significant relations with the middle-level managers' perception on the internal organizational environment. However, although the correlations are very weak, these have a negative value, which means that with the increase of both the time in the organization and time in the position, the perceptions of managers with respect to the internal organizational environment tend to decrease.

The Kruskal–Wallis test application showed that, regarding the size of the organization, there are no statistically significant differences in the perception of intermediate-level managers in relation to the organization's internal environment ($\chi^2 (3) = 4.684$, $p = 0.196$). However, small companies are those with higher levels of perception (*mean rank* = 41.23) and large companies are those with lower levels of perception (*mean rank* = 25.00).

Student's *t* test application showed that there is no significant difference in the perception on the internal organizational environment between managers of the industry and trade/services areas ($t(64) = -0.765$, $p = 0.448 > 0.05$). From the sampling point of view, it can be stated that managers who perform functions in the area of trade/services activity ($M = 3.38$; $SD = 0.48$) have the highest levels of perception when compared to industry ($M = 3.26$; $SD = 0.74$).

Conclusions

The present work allows us to make a reading about some internal conditions that influence the participation of middle-level managers in Portugal for the entrepreneurship activities' promotion.

According to the results, we can infer that if top management, on the one hand, favors a supportive climate that allows mid-level managers to facilitate and promote entrepreneurial activities, on the other hand, they condition that same support to (1) not provide promotions and rewards following the development of new and innovative ideas and (2) not making funds available for new projects.

This comportment suggests a lack of strategic entrepreneurial vision and an organizational architecture that stimulates entrepreneurial processes and behaviors. However, for the performance of their duties, middle-level managers, especially SMEs managers, have autonomy and flexibility in the management of their work processes and the decision-making of their tasks.

We also conclude that rewards/reinforcement, whether for performance or recognition of effort, are not a practice predominantly valued by organizations.

As advocated by Alpkan et al. (2010), it is an important time to imagine, observe, experiment, and develop new ideas. However, the results obtained point to the short time available by intermediate-level managers for these practices. This limitation can be seen in aspects such as (1) the possibility of developing intrapreneurial ideas and activities, (2) a limitation of available resources for innovation, and (3) top management's attention and support for promising innovative ideas.

Finally, it should be noted that this assessment tool (CEAI), because of its easy application and interpretation with respect to the results, should be considered as relevant in the management function, as it gives top managers a concise and directed script in the sense of encouraging entrepreneurship activities and measuring individual entrepreneurship behaviors.

References

Alpkan, L., Bulut, C., Gunday, G., Ulusoy, G. and Kilic, K. (2010) 'Organizational support for intrapreneurship and its interaction with human capital to enhance innovative performance', *Management Decision*, 48(6): 732–755.

Antoncic, B. and Hisrich, R. D. (2001) 'Intrapreneurship: construct refinement and cross-cultural validation', *Journal of Business Venturing*, 16(5): 495–527.

Barringer, B. and Bluedorn, A. (1999) 'The relationship between corporate entrepreneurship and strategic management', *Strategic Management Journal*, 20: 421–444.

Brown, T., Davidsson, P. and Wiklund, J. (2001) 'An operationalization of Stevenson's conceptualization of entrepreneurship as opportunity-based firm behavior', *Strategic Management Journal*, 22(10): 953–968.

Covin, J., Green, K. and Slevin, D. (2006) 'Strategic process effects on the entrepreneurial orientation sales growth rate relationship', *Entrepreneurship Theory and Practice*, 30(3): 57–82.

Covin, J. and Slevin, D. (1991) 'A conceptual model of entrepreneurship as firm behavior', *Entrepreneurship: Theory and Practice*, 16(1): 7–24.

Dess, G., Ireland, R., Zahra, S., Floyd, S., Janney, J. and Lane, P. (2003) 'Emerging issues in corporate entrepreneurship', *Journal of Management*, 29(3): 351–378.

Floyd, S. and Lane, P. (2000) 'Strategizing throughout the organization: managing role conflict in strategic renewal', *Academy of Management Review*, 25(1): 154–177.

Floyd, S. and Wooldridge, B. (1992) 'Middle management involvement in strategy and its association with strategic type: A research note', *Strategic Management Journal*, 13: 153–167.

Foba, T. and De Villiers, D. (2007) 'The integration of intrapreneurship into a performance management model', *Journal of Human Resource Management*, 5(2): 1–8.

Goldsby, M., Kuratko, D., Hornsby, J., Houghton, J. and Neck, C. (2006) 'Social cognition and corporate entrepreneurship: A framework for enhancing the role of middle-level managers', *International Journal of Leadership Studies*, 2(1): 17–35.

Hayton, J. and Kelley, D. (2006) 'A competency-based framework for promoting corporate entrepreneurship', *Human Resource Management*, 45(3): 407–427.

Hitt, M., Ireland, R., Sirmon, D. and Trahms, C. (2011) 'Strategic entrepreneurship: Creating value for individuals, organizations, and society', *The Academy of Management Perspective*, 25(2): 57–75.

Hornsby, J., Kuratko, D., Shepherd, D. and Bott, J. (2009) 'Managers' corporate entrepreneurial actions: Examining perception and position', *Journal of Business Venturing*, 24(3): 236–247.

Hornsby, J., Kuratko, D. and Zahra, S. (2002) 'Middle manager's perception of the internal environment for corporate entrepreneurship: Assessing a measurement scale', *Journal of Business Venturing*, 17: 253–273.

Ireland, D., Covin, J. and Kuratko, D. (2009) 'Conceptualizing corporate entrepreneurship strategy', *Entrepreneurship Theory and Practice*, 33(1): 19–46.

Kuratko, D., Hornsby, J. and Bishop, J. (2005) 'Managers corporate entrepreneurial actions and job satisfaction', *International Entrepreneurship and Management Journal*, 1(3): 275–291.

Lumpkin, G. and Dess, G. (1996) 'Clarifying the entrepreneurial orientation construct and linking it to performance', *Academy of Management Review*, 21(1): 135–172.

Lumpkin, G. and Dess, G. (2001) 'Linking two dimensions of entrepreneurial orientation to firm performance: The moderating role of environment and industry life cycle', *Journal of Business Venturing*, 16(3): 429–451.

Marvel, M., Griffin, A., Hebda, J. and Vojak, B. (2007) 'Examining the technical corporate entrepreneurs' motivation: Voices from the field', *Entrepreneurship Theory and Practice*, 31(5): 753–768.

Pestana, M. and Gageiro, J. (2014) *Análise de dados em Ciências Sociais – A complementaridade do SPSS*, 6th ed. Lisboa: Editora Sílabo.

Sarkar, S. (2014) *Empreendedorismo e Inovação*, 3rd ed. Lisboa: Escolar Editora.

Schein, E. (1992) *Organizational culture and leadership*, 2nd ed. San Francisco: Jossey-Bass Publishers.

Zahra, S. (1991) 'Predictors and financial outcomes of corporate entrepreneurship: An exploratory study', *Journal of Business Venturing*, 6(4): 259–285.

Zahra, S. (1993) 'A conceptual model of entrepreneurship as firm behavior: A critique and extension', *Entrepreneurship: Theory and Practice*, 17(4): 5–21.

8 Building and maintaining customer relationship via digital marketing and new technologies for small businesses during the COVID-19 pandemic

Esha Thukral and Vanessa Ratten

Introduction

Digital transformation is pushing businesses to change their business models and constantly reevaluate their ongoing operations and adapt to the new market realities. Digitalization has radically changed our working world and will continue to do so. Today, emails are a predominant mode of day-to-day communication instead of classical letters. Technologies are becoming more and more equipped in recognizing speech, emotions, and gestures paving the way for people to communicate with machines intuitively (Hippmann, Klingner and Leis, 2019). Thus, digital technologies are now transforming customer lifestyle and habits.

Businesses are built on relationships, as two-thirds of a company's competitive advantage comes from its customer experience (Morgan, 2019). The more one communicates with the consumers and solves their issues, the more loyal customers become, and having loyal customers is one of the biggest assets for any business as they are the source of continuous revenue generation for a business. Therefore, businesses too, are incorporating technology to establish customer relationships to suit the consumer lifestyle and habits.

Customer relationship management (CRM) is a sum of all the activities, strategies, and technologies that a business uses to interact with the current as well as potential consumers. CRM not only assists companies in creating customer loyalties and enhancing customer satisfaction but also efficiency and profits (Kulpa, 2017). Therefore, the service and relationship marketing literature has for long recognized the importance of managing and developing customer relationships, and research on customer loyalty, customer perceived service, customer satisfaction, etc., is extensive (Heinonen and Michelsson, 2010). However, there is limited research on building customer relations in a digital context as technologies are continuously evolving and its uses are continuously explored.

A whirlwind of disruptive digital forces is in play

'The customer is King' has been the popular mantra in the marketing and sales department and so to ignore the disruptive forces in action when the rules of customer engagement/relationship are changing would not be a strategic move on the part of businesses. Therefore, to continue attracting and retaining the customers, businesses need to recognize these changing dynamics and adapt accordingly.

Four major forces that are changing the business environment are: (Deloitte Digital, 2019)

Customer demographics and behavior: Customer behaviors have radically changed especially within the last decade. Companies too have to keep pace with the changing behaviors and preferences of the customers and adapt their marketing and sales strategy accordingly to meet the changing needs of the consumers. Contemporary consumers are well informed (e.g., online comparison sites, peer validation, and smart recommenders), fast-paced, picky (rely on online reviews), always connected (uses smartphones, wearables, and corresponding technology at all times), tech-savvy. There is a strong desire for self-service, e.g., they want the convenience to access relevant information without a customer service representative, but also expert consulting once they need it. Thus, they demand more than just goods and services, they are looking for experiences, and convenience.

*New business models:*As customers' expectations and behavior changes, companies too experiment with new business models to create new revenue streams. Some well-known examples include Spotify using the Freemium business model, Netflix using revenue models through relatively low monthly subscriptions. In both the aforementioned businesses, model's continuous customer engagement is needed to generate a sustainable revenue stream and turning recent adopters to loyal customers. If for any reason customer expectations are not met, they are most likely to leave the company. Therefore, building long-lasting relationship with customers is crucial.

*Technological advances:*Technology is at the heart of Digital Customer relationship management. Technology is integral to meeting the evolving needs and expectations of customers. These days consumers prefer personalized services that make life easier and seamless. To provide personalized services, advanced computing techniques can be used to harness volumes of personal data (e.g., search, social, geo-tagged sensors, payments, shopping carts, speech) to create the magic behind new hyper-personalized experiences (Accenture, 2017).

*The Desire for Transparency:*Over the years, the marketing budget has increased substantially and is further expected to increase, since the priority of traditional media decreases, more than 50% of the marketing budgets are expected to be spent on digital marketing by 2023. The increase in marketing budget will eventually put more pressure on the top management who are responsible for overall customer experience to justify their growing expenditure and provide transparency about the return on investment. Customer relationship management leaders will be relying more on digital communication channels to be able to generate reliable, valuable customer data, and establish advanced analytics capabilities to demonstrate the effectiveness of CRM measures (Deloitte Digital, 2019).

Organizations and marketers need to take account of the disruptive forces in action and channel it to their advantage and stay at the leading edge of emerging technologies. Businesses need to incorporate technology and use it as a competitive advantage like Netflix defeated Blockbuster in the chase of market share just by adopting the change, similarly, Amazon.com changing the way we buy books and thus disrupting distribution channel by introducing Kindle. Marketers who are averse to change or are not ready to adapt and use new technology will be left behind in the chase of market share (Petersen, Person and Nash, The Customer is in Control, 2014).

Since the change is inevitable, the need of the hour is to have an agile marketing approach, this enables the organizations to review the performance of the campaign frequently and iterate accordingly. According to the article published by Mckinsey & Company, 'Agile, in the marketing context, means using data and analytics to continuously source promising opportunities or solutions to problems in real-time, deploying tests quickly, evaluating the results, and rapidly iterating' (Edelman, Heller and Spittaels, 2016).

Digital strategy a clear winner during COVID-19

In a very short period, COVID-19 has overwhelmed our lives and livelihoods. The pandemic has caused disruptions to many businesses across the globe due to lockdown and social distancing measures. On the one hand, some companies had to completely stop their operations, such as movie theaters and tourism operators. Whereas others had to alter their business practices by adopting 'work from home' as the new normal (Meyer, 2020). When people all over the world are in isolation, avoiding in-person contact, businesses will have to become more and more reliant on digital technology and digital strategy to establish contact with the customers. Digital mode is a clear winner, especially now as COVID-19 has created a new normal marked by, social distancing and self-isolation.

Due to COVID-19 prospective, customers are less open to the idea of meeting face to face, and everyone is clueless as to when things will go back to normal or whether this will lead to a long-term change. The world we live in is characterized by uncertainty, fluidity, and change; therefore, resilient business strategies are essential for a road to economic/business recovery and a key factor in resilience is adaptability. Adapting may mean exploring new channels over the web or social media platforms where introductions can be made, and customer relationships can be fostered. And as long as businesses create an appropriate action plan and robust digital marketing strategy, there is no reason why it should just serve as an emergency fill-in but could continue to provide long-term value when the world eventually gets back to normal (Marr, 2020).

This is already reflecting in China, where 55% of customers are intending to permanently shift to e-commerce (Diebner, Silliman, Ungerman and Vancauwenberghe, 2020).

Sitecore: customer experience maturity model

As customers are becoming more tech savvy, they expect the same from the businesses. To establish customer loyalty an appropriate action plan is needed. A proactive approach would be to use the customer experience maturity model by Sitecore as a framework for determining the current stage where customers fall and accordingly setting goals for future improvement. The model not only acknowledges the value of creating long-term customer relationship but also takes into account that maturity level of the customers (as customers are more mature/informed in terms of shopping than they were before). The model identifies three levels of customer maturity: attract, convert, and advocate, and seven strategies initiate, radiate, align, optimize, nurture, engage, and lifetime customer that span the cycle from new customer to lifetime loyal customer.

Attract

Initiate

The main objectives at the initiation stage are:

- To create a web/online presence with all the general information about the company.
- Focus is on search engine optimization to attract more visitors.

Radiate

The main objectives of the Radiate stage are:

- To expand the organization's digital presence across various channels.
- Reach customers through social media channels with context-appropriate content

(Petersen, Person and Nash, Stage 1-Initiate
and Stage 2-Radiate, 2014).

Align

The Align stage objectives are:

- Demonstrate how digital goals drive strategic as well as marketing objectives. At this stage, the content becomes focused on customer behavior.
- Create an Engagement Value Scale (EVS) that measures whether a marketing effort has successfully penetrated/attracted the customers. For example,

a campaign or a page that has garnered high engagement value has a high relevance/importance to customers

(Petersen, Person and Nash, Stage 3-Align, 2014).

Convert

Optimize

The main objectives of this stage are:

- Optimize your digital presence to get higher engagement by focusing on creating relevant experiences for the customer (use personalization). Personalization includes many tactics; it can be as simple as using customer names after they log in.
- Optimize marketing efforts by measuring marketing performances across channels

(Petersen, Person and Nash, Stage 4-Optimize, 2014).

Nurture

The key objectives of this stage are:

- Evolve from multichannel to cross channel communication with a customer-centric, approach, digitally listening to the behavior of the customers, and responding in individual customers' preferred channels like behavioral targeting. It is a technique which is used in online advertising wherein data from visitors browsing pattern are used to display relevant advertisements, offers, and campaigns.
- Make considerable use of automated channels and personalized email marketing. For example, reminding the customer about abandoned shopping cart, etc.

(Petersen, Person and Nash, Stage 5-Nurture, 2014).

Advocate

Engage

The Engage stage objectives are:
- Integrate both online and offline data by creating a central repository via Cloud. It helps in giving a holistic view of each customer. This helps in enhancing the quality of customer communication and responsiveness. It further supports a customer-centric technique to help prioritize sales and marketing strategy when dealing with different customer groups. This information can then be used to manage, measure, and keep track of marketing, sales, and customer service activities as they relate to the customer. Overall, it builds greater customer loyalty and better customer experience.

(Petersen, Person and Nash, Stage 6-Engage, 2014).

Lifetime customer

The main objectives of this stage are:

- Creating an exceptional customer experience so that customers' loyalty can be established.
- Use real-time data to anticipate customers' action and needs to enhance customer experience.
- Maintain the competitive advantage by being the fastest, agile, and adaptable in testing new initiatives.

> For example, Amazon filed a patent for a predictive analytics system that predicts what product purchases are likely to be made in the near future in a specific area. This enables it to ship items to the specific area and reduce delivery cost and arrival time.
>
> (Petersen, Person and Nash, Stage 7-Lifetime Customers, 2014).

The importance of using an appropriate model cannot be overlooked in establishing customer relations or enhancing customer experiences, whether it is the aforementioned model or any other model. It helps a business in assessing which stage their customers fall and accordingly design a future path for themselves and their customers. The model provides the leader of the organization with the compass, map, and an engine to get to their destination, which is enhanced customer relationship. However, without a model organization's effort will be scattered and disjointed, leading to no definitive outcome.

Case examples to build customer relationship via new technologies

In the digital age, customer experiences affect customer retention rates and eventually help build long-term customer relations. Businesses are using various ways/modes to connect with customers. Below are some of the case examples to build customer relationship via new technologies:

> ***Digital presence: Meet your customers where they are:*** Customers are experiencing a new normal where it is impossible to conduct activities in a normal fashion, like dining out with friends and a trip to the grocery store are either prohibited or is risky. Consumer needs have shifted and it can be supported by statistics. Online penetration in China has risen by 15–20%. E-commerce sale in Italy has gone up 80% in a single week. Demand and popularity for digital experiences will continue to increase, and businesses who act promptly and innovate their business models to help customers navigate through the crisis will eventually gain a strong competitive advantage over others. In the

new normal, it is not just about the company's digital presence it is also about providing a great customer service experience to its customers (Diebner et al., 2020). Amazon is an excellent example of e-commerce model. It not only meets the need of the customers by having an extended market reach as they sell a variety of products like apparels, footwear, health products, etc. but also provides personalized shopping experience to its customers by using data to track their behavioral pattern.

Social media presence: Customer relationship management is about getting closer to the customer by staying in touch, and Social media platforms present opportunities to engage with the customers. Social media is the most efficient channel to distribute information, promote products or services, and expand the consumer base. Customers like to socialize, exchange information/ideas over social networks, and the information/ideas shared by the customers can be used by companies to develop products that better satisfy the need and wants of the clients (Elena, 2016). PlayStation has a whooping following on Twitter. It is one of the most followed brands. According to UnMetric, PlayStation has seen 376% growth in followers in the past 5 years alone from 2014 to 2019, 12 million followers have joined. One of the reasons is that the brand is quite active on the platform, regularly posting content to engage the followers, launching game trailers, streaming live events. Even during COVID-19, the brand garnered some positive image with its **#PlayAtHome** campaign, motivating users to stay at home by downloading its 'Unchartered: The Nathan Drake Collection' and 'Journey' games for free and almost ten million people did download (Gilliland, 2020).

*Chatbots:*They are powered by artificial intelligence that can understand the queries of the customers and answer accordingly. It is like an automated conversation system, which has become increasingly sophisticated. When a business is considering a decision to use chatbots or virtual agents, business leaders must examine what kind of companies are best served by chatbots, and how to integrate them into their existing customer service system. For companies that deal with a large volume of customer service requests for them the effect of using Chatbots can be huge, this way companies can improve their service levels, as bots are available 24/7 and are faster at answering customer queries than humans (Kannan and Bernoff, 2019). The global chatbot market is expected to reach $1.23 billion by 2025. Numerous companies are using Chatbots and have been successful in engaging customers. Companies that use Chatbots successfully are Dominos, Starbucks, Sephora, and many others.

Sephora, the retail store, uses chatbots to improve customer service. After the success of their app through Kik (messaging app), they have now introduced some additional interactive features in the app to further enhance the customer experience. The two services that they have introduced are

Sephora Reservation Assistant: This enables the customer to interact and make an appointment with the beauty specialists by sending a message to the chatbot. The chatbot is equipped with smart learning capability, which makes interaction smooth as the chatbot understands the language used by the customer to make interaction easier (conversational commerce).

Sephora Color Match: It uses augmented reality to help customers choose the colors. The user will have to simply hold and face the camera, and the shade will be selected for the user from the Sephora line of products. It can also help match cosmetics with the outfit of the user.

*Augmented Reality:*It embeds virtual objects in real environments. Augmented reality is set to be a $50 billion industry by 2024. It can allow customers to try products before they purchase them (Business.com, 2020). Gucci added an augmented reality feature to its application where the user can point the app at their feet, which will enable them to see Gucci sneakers on their feet (Kaplan, 2020).

Conclusion

To conclude, it can be said that businesses must shift to the practice of experience marketing. This simply means to always take into account the forces of change in play (digitalization or emerging new technologies, changing customer behavior/motivation) and constantly adapt and align marketing strategies and content continuously to enhance customer relationship. Thus, businesses should use an agile approach to maintain a competitive advantage.

References

Accenture. (2017) *Dynamic digital consumers: Ever changing expectations & technology intrigue*, www.accenture.com/us-en/_acnmedia/PDF-39/Accenture-PoV-Dynamic-Consumers. pdf, last visited 2nd September 2020.

Business.com. (2020) *Tech industry analysts and visionaries say augmented reality will revolutionize business*, www.business.com/articles/best-augmented-reality-uses/, last visited 4th September 2020.

Deloitte Digital. (2019) *Digital CRM 2.0 Building customer relationships in the digital landscape*. Melbourne, Australia: Deloitte.

Diebner, R., Silliman, E., Ungerman, K. and Vancauwenberghe, M. (2020) *Adapting customer experience in the time of coronavirus*, www.mckinsey.com/business-functions/marketing-and-sales/our-insights/adapting-customer-experience-in-the-time-of-coronavirus, last visited 3rd September 2020.

Edelman, D., Heller, J. and Spittaels, S. (2016) *Agile marketing: A step-by-step guide. McKinsey insights*. Boston: McKinsey.

Elena, C. A. (2016) 'Social media – A strategy in developing customer relationship management', *Procedia Economics and Finance*, 39: 785–790.

Gilliland, N. (2020) *30 brands with excellent social media strategies*, https://econsultancy.com/30-brands-with-excellent-social-media-strategies/, last visited 4th September 2020.

Heinonen, K. and Michelsson, T. (2010) 'The use of digital channels to create customer relationships', *International Journal of Internet Marketing and Advertising*, 10: 1–20.

Hippmann, D. S., Klingner, D. and Leis, D. (2019) 'Digitization – Areas of application and research objectives', In R. Neugebauer (Ed.), *Digital transformation* (pp. 9–17). Heidelberg: Springer.

Kannan, P. and Bernoff, J. (2019) *Does your company really need a chatbot?*, https://hbr.org/2019/05/does-your-company-really-need-a-chatbot, last visited 4th September 2020.

Kaplan, N. (2020) *How companies are using digital tools to build customer relationships*, www.forbes.com/sites/forbestechcouncil/2020/07/13/how-companies-are-using-digital-tools-to-build-customer-relationships/#798795321101, last visited 4th September 2020.

Kulpa, J. (2017) *Why is customer relationship management so important?*, www.forbes.com/sites/forbesagencycouncil/2017/10/24/why-is-customer-relationship-management-so-important/#1fdb2b287dac, last visited 2nd September 2020.

Marr, B. (2020) *Why companies turn to digital marketing to survive Covid-19*, www.forbes.com/sites/bernardmarr/2020/03/20/why-companies-turn-to-digital-marketing-to-survive-covid-19/#2f415d062425, last visited 3rd September 2020.

Meyer, K. (2020) *The coronavirus crisis: A catalyst for entrepreneurship*, https://theconversation.com/the-coronavirus-crisis-a-catalyst-for-entrepreneurship-135005, last visited 3rd September 2020.

Morgan, B. (2019) *100 stats on digital transformation and customer experience*, www.forbes.com/sites/blakemorgan/2019/12/16/100-stats-on-digital-transformation-and-customer-experience/#3235613f3bf3, last visited 4th September 2020.

Petersen, L. B., Person, R. and Nash, C. (2014) 'The customer is in control', In *Connect: How to use data and experience marketing to create lifetime customers* (pp. 1–8). New York: John Wiley & Sons.

Petersen, L. B., Person, R. and Nash, C. (2014) 'Stage 1-Initiate and Stage 2-Radiate', In *Connect: How to use data and experience marketing to create lifetime customers* (pp. 66–90). New York: John Wiley & Sons.

Petersen, L. B., Person, R. and Nash, C. (2014) 'Stage 3-Align', In *Connect: How to use data and experience marketing to create lifetime customers* (pp. 91–121). New York: John Wiley & Sons.

Petersen, L. B., Person, R. and Nash, C. (2014) 'Stage 4-Optimize', In *Connect: How to use data and experience marketing to create lifetime customers* (pp. 122–152). New York: John Wiley & Sons.

Petersen, L. B., Person, R. and Nash, C. (2014) 'Stage 5-Nurture', In *Connect: How to use data and experience marketing to create lifetime customers* (pp. 153–175). New York: John Wiley & Sons.

Petersen, L. B., Person, R. and Nash, C. (2014) 'Stage 6-Engage', In *Connect: How to use data and experience marketing to create lifetime customers* (pp. 176–197). New York: John Wiley & Sons.

Petersen, L. B., Person, R. and Nash, C. (2014) 'Stage 7-Lifetime customers', In *Connect: How to use data and experience marketing to create lifetime customers* (pp. 198–219). New York: John Wiley & Sons.

9 The future of small business entrepreneurship based on COVID-19 change

Vanessa Ratten

Introduction

COVID-19 research is challenging due to the ongoing and complex nature of the health pandemic (Cortez and Johnston, 2020). Entrepreneurship is perceived in both positive and negative ways in times of crisis. From a positive view, entrepreneurship brings much-needed change required for businesses to continue operating in changed environmental conditions (Ferreira, Fernandes and Ratten, 2017). This means entrepreneurs bring a sense of relief to the current conditions faced by citizens by enabling new products and services to emerge in the marketplace. On the flipside, there are negative effects of COVID-19 entrepreneurship due to the price gauging and manipulation of markets. This means some entrepreneurs emerge stronger in times of crisis due to their ability to access specific resources namely finance and human capital (Ferreira, Fayolle, Ratten and Raposo, 2018). However, it can be a struggle for small business entrepreneurs in a crisis as they are reliant on local areas for business activity. While some can change to offering their products and services on an online platform, not all can do this. This is due to human-to-human interaction needed by small businesses particularly those in the beauty, tourism, and entertainment industries.

A deeper understanding about the role entrepreneurship has played during the COVID-19 pandemic is required to take into consideration new market conditions (Eggers, 2020). There currently is a dearth of empirical evidence about the role of entrepreneurship in the COVID-19 pandemic. This means scholars and practitioners lack a robust understanding about how to measure the impact of entrepreneurship during times of crisis. In addition, extant research has not specifically examined how the context of COVID-19 has influenced entrepreneurial intentions. This means while the practice of entrepreneurship is well known in times of crisis, there is a lack of theoretically relevant relationships between the experience of entrepreneurs and business ventures associated with crises.

The topic of COVID-19 and small business entrepreneurship is still nascent and more research is needed to better explain the phenomenon. The impact of COVID-19 on entrepreneurship varies widely in terms of impact and outcomes. These changes can be considered through both social and economic effects (He and Harris, 2020). Social effects relate to the changing work and lifestyle conditions required by the COVID-19 crisis. Economic effects refer to the monetary and financial implications of the COVID-19 crisis. Both types of effect are relevant to understanding the linkage between COVID-19 and entrepreneurship but despite the existing entrepreneurship research being rich in content it lacks a COVID-19 perspective. This means the entrepreneurship resulting from COVID-19 changes has the potential to enrich the emerging work on different fields of entrepreneurship in a number of ways. This includes (1) what drives entrepreneurship in times of crisis, (2) organization of new enterprises, (3) internationalization of ideas, and (4) outcomes of entrepreneurship.

In this chapter, potential research ideas will be discussed in light of the COVID-19 pandemic. This will include specific research opportunities related to different areas of entrepreneurship. In addition, general issues and considerations about COVID-19 will be discussed. As with all research agendas regarding entrepreneurship these ideas are not meant to be exhaustive but rather serve as starting points for new research paths. Therefore, this chapter provides an overview of the literature on COVID-19 and entrepreneurship in an effort to address this important research area of inquiry. To do this, the chapter discusses what is currently known about COVID-19 entrepreneurship and then identifies research gaps. This provides a way to close the current lack of understanding about COVID-19 entrepreneurship by prioritizing new research lines of inquiry.

COVID-19 and societal change

Society has recovered from previous crises in different ways. Natural disasters such as hurricanes and earthquakes have resulted in changes to building codes and the use of manufacturing equipment (Hills, 1998). Other disasters such as famine and war have resulted in changed migration patterns and increased emphasis on quality of life. Therefore, the way society responds to the COVID-19 crisis is unknown due to its effect being felt at a social, economic, and psychological level (Hall, Scott and Gössling, 2020). Socially individuals have had to socially distance, which has resulted in increased feelings of isolation. Economically many businesses have had to close or substantially alter the way they conduct business transactions. Psychologically there has been an increase in anxiety and depression resulting from the crisis. Each of these effects is relevant for entrepreneurs who are key drivers of the recovery as they respond to social change by providing solutions.

In the past decade, research combining entrepreneurship with other areas of study have flourished (Jones, Jones, Williams-Burnett and Ratten, 2017). This means there is a natural progression for entrepreneurship studies to be integrated into other research areas. Due to the impact of COVID-19 on the global economy, it seems that there is a need to integrate more of an entrepreneurship perspective into COVID-19 research. Analyzing how businesses have reacted to the crisis in an entrepreneurial way can provide a unique way to build knowledge. This is important as the effects of the COVID-19 crisis on businesses have been unprecedented. The COVID-19 crisis has caused painful disruptions in the way life is conducted (Kraus, Clauss, Breier, Gast, Zardini and

Tiberius, 2020). The rules around business changed that resulted in a massive shift toward digital transactions. Not all businesses could change or adapt due to the type of commerce they were engaged in. This meant some businesses have struggled to survive with many businesses failing. Moreover, the crisis has caused trauma much in the same way that previous crises like the September 11, 2001, terrorism attacks and the 2008 Global Financial Crisis (Buchanan and Denyer, 2013). As a result, businesses have had to shift their business models to new sources of competitive advantage. To do this has been hard as the shift was done in a short time period with few alternatives available.

Businesses have had to think entrepreneurially to seek out new opportunities and to devise innovative management techniques due to the crisis (Doern, 2016). An example of this is with restaurants that had to close their in-house dining due to COVID-19 restrictions and move to takeaway and home delivery services. At the same time, these businesses had difficulties with their supply chain due to it being hard to source timely materials. In addition, due to travel restrictions and the lockdown provisions, restaurants have had to rely on the materials available (Kuckertz, Brändle, Gaudig, Hinderer, Reyes, Prochotta and Berger, 2020). This has meant behaving in an entrepreneurial manner in order to continue their business operations. Examples of change include restaurants offering curbside delivery and click and collect services. In addition, take-home cooking kits provided a new source of revenue for individuals at home who had more time to cook. Due to the concurrent impacts on the delivery of services and geographic restrictions, many businesses were not adequately prepared for the change resulting from the COVID-19 crisis (Donthu and Gustafsson, 2020).

It is believed that a vaccine is required before the world moves back to pre-pandemic normalcy (Marshall and Wolanskyj-Spinner, 2020). There is a belief that a vaccine will be found; however, when this occurs is still unknown. Moreover, who will get access to this vaccine is being debated due to profit versus public health interests. Jeyanathan, Afkhami, Smaill, Miller, Lichty and Xing (2020:616) state the six major types of candidate vaccine for the COVID-19 disease are 'live attenuated virus, recombinant viral vectored, inactivated virus, protein subunit, virus-like particles and nucleic acid based.' The race for a vaccine has raised a number of ethical questions about the proper testing and timeframes required. In addition, there are political pressures around obtaining a vaccine in relation to the November 2020 U.S. election. Therefore, COVID-19 is considered as being one of the most formidable challenges to business. The COVID-19 crisis has brought business to a standstill with many not knowing how they should change (Parnell, Widdop, Bond and Wilson, 2020). The ongoing and indeterminate time frame of the virus makes it even harder for businesses to plan for the future. This is important in the world environment that has most countries implementing restricted movement policies that were previously not considered as a possibility (Wen, Wang, Kozak, Liu and Hou, 2020). In the past, there was a continual upward trend in international travel and movement, which has been significantly curtailed due to the virus. The concept of 'over tourism' has now changed to 'no tourism' that reflects a major paradigm shift (Higgins-Desbiolles, 2020). Due to the new nature of the COVID-19 disease, it is unclear which vaccine strategy will work, which has meant a number of potential vaccines have been developed (Kirk and Rifkin, 2020). Due to the concurrent need to find a vaccine but also manage the new market environment there is a need to discover new perspectives for small business entrepreneurs.

Need for new perspectives in future research directions

The topic of COVID-19 entrepreneurship is still nascent and more research is required to understand the phenomenon. COVID-19 entrepreneurship varies widely in terms of its origins, characteristics, and outcomes. In addition, there are both social and financial goals to consider in any form of entrepreneurship (Jones, Klapper, Ratten and Fayolle, 2018). The entrepreneurship literature is rich in theory and empirical data, but is only recently focusing on COVID-19-related topics. This means existing entrepreneurship research offers promising areas for future research that integrates COVID-19 information into entrepreneurship studies. Existing entrepreneurship frameworks might not necessarily be able to integrate a COVID-19 approach so new theories may need to be created. Alternatively, existing theories such as crisis management might be used by adjusting to the COVID-19 context (Ansell and Boin, 2019).

The diversity characterizing the entrepreneurship literature can be of greater benefit to COVID-19 research. Existing studies on entrepreneurship draw from many fields including behavioral sciences, economics, and management science (Ratten, 2017). This means new research on COVID-19 entrepreneurship can follow the same interdisciplinary path but broaden the focus to incorporate more applicability to crisis management. Therefore, some relaxing some of the existing theoretical assumptions can be conducted by suggesting new approaches such as social interest and a need to manage change to suit the COVID-19 context (Brinks and Ibert, 2020). The next sections will further discuss specific future research topics related to COVID-19, small business, and entrepreneurship.

Context

COVID-19 entrepreneurship is highly influenced by contextual settings so it is suggested that future research considers different contextual settings (Brown and Rocha, 2020). This can be achieved by utilizing theoretical frameworks in existing entrepreneurship studies such as the theory of planned behavior or theory of knowledge spillovers then applying it to the COVID-19 context. The context in which the COVID-19 occurs can be characterized by enterprise-level factors such as business strategy and an extreme level of uncertainty (Bailey and Breslin, 2020). This would enable research to focus on how COVID-19 entrepreneurship is based on firm conditions and how this determines performance.

There are numerous possibilities for carrying out more research regarding the process of COVID-19 entrepreneurship. This would enable a better understanding about the patterns emerging from different contexts based on

Table 9.1 Potential context research avenues based on the contextualization of COVID-19 entrepreneurship research

Type of context	Examples
Social	How individuals change their social interactions based on relational embeddedness.
	The role of religion and spirituality in dealing with the crisis.
	Reconfiguration of social relationships resulting from environmental change.
	Impact of working from home on social relationships.
	Faith and trust in public health responses to the COVID-19 crisis.
Spatial	Difference between urban and rural forms of COVID-19 entrepreneurship.
	Government policy initiatives regarding the response to COVID-19.
	The use of clusters to encourage geographically motivated COVID-19 entrepreneurship.
Temporal	Impact of time on COVID-19 entrepreneurship.
	Whether the rates of infection influence the type of COVID-19 entrepreneurship.
	How entrepreneurial ecosystems involving COVID-19 innovation evolve.
	Impact of digital transformation on COVID-19 entrepreneurship.

Source: Author developed

their applicability to finding solutions related to the COVID-19 crisis (Brammer and Clark, 2020). Industry settings are a context that should be further examined in entrepreneurship studies (Jones, Ratten, Klapper and Fayolle, 2019). COVID-19 entrepreneurial activities are affected by the industry in which they take place. Some industries such as education might be more open to entrepreneurial possibilities due to the impact of COVID-19 on business (Krishnamurthy, 2020). This means industries such as education, health, and sport need to be separately studied in detail. Moreover, context can be considered in terms of social, spatial, and temporal conditions. Future research ideas based on these contexts are explained more in Table 9.1.

Methodology

New methodologies need to be considered in future research regarding COVID-19, entrepreneurship, and small business. Studies related to COVID-19 entrepreneurship at the moment have tended to be based on cross-sectional data without considering more long-term effects. While this is to be expected, given the relatively recent nature of the crisis, future research needs to be built on more robust research methodologies (Ratten and Jones, 2018). This means utilizing a mixed-methods approach to analyze the data on COVID-19 entrepreneurship in different ways. Both qualitative and quantitative data should be acquired about any crisis that enables a more holistic understanding about its impact on entrepreneurship.

Research on COVID-19 entrepreneurship has attracted much attention especially in methodology circles. Despite its popularity, the concept suffers from a number of shortcomings due to its nascent nature: (1) it lacks a clear definition that makes its conceptualization easy to understand, (2) does not yet have a theoretical framework to understand its key elements, and (3) it remains a challenge to differentiate it from other forms of entrepreneurship. For each of these shortcomings, new research is required to provide a number of suggestions.

The COVID-19 entrepreneurship literature aims to explain entrepreneurship from a COVID-19 perspective. This is an ambitious goal due to the current and ongoing nature of the health pandemic (Akkermans, Richardson and Kraimer, 2020). It is a rapidly growing literature that will shape how we look at crises in the future. Despite its practical relevance, scholars have used different expressions in the past when analyzing disaster management (Faulkner, 2001). While the expressions have similar meanings, they utilize different theoretical and methodological frameworks. At the moment, the current body of literature on COVID-19 entrepreneurship suffers a number of shortcomings in that (1) what is its cause and effect is unknown, (2) the elements of COVID-19 entrepreneurship are unclear, and (3) the evolutionary nature of COVID-19 has not been considered. Therefore, future research needs to consider collecting data from different industries, geographical, and time periods in order to better understand its effects on entrepreneurship.

The main topic in the COVID-19 entrepreneurship literature is the mix of social and financial objectives in business decisions. The lack of large-scale data about COVID-19 entrepreneurship is a handicap. This might change as more data related to the impact of COVID-19 on business are collected (Alon, Farrell and Li, 2020). Creating new and detailed data sources is an important way to move the field of COVID-19 entrepreneurship further (Liguori and Winkler, 2020). This involves collecting global datasets on COVID-19 entrepreneurship. While qualitative data have an important place in entrepreneurship studies, there is a simultaneous need for quantitative data. This will enable the nuances and theoretical drivers of COVID-19 entrepreneurship to be explored in more detail. I hope that besides advancing the current literature and practice on COVID-19 entrepreneurship will also further stimulate interest in this topic.

The exact impact of COVID-19 on entrepreneurship is still unknown due to its recent and ongoing nature. This means the literature has not yet documented or explained the effects of the COVID-19 pandemic on entrepreneurship. While in practice the impact of the COVID-19 pandemic can be seen by the altered workplace practices, the academic literature is still somewhat behind. This practice–academic gap is natural in research on crisis management given the time it takes to report research findings (Liu, Shankar and Yun, 2017). The emerging COVID-19 literature has explored the immediate impact of the crisis, but more long-term effects are still unknown. This has meant most data tend to be short-term oriented and focused on one industry. Industry comparative data taken at different time points are still lacking. Moreover, the emerging literature has not yet compared and contrasted different response mechanisms used by governments to control the spread of the virus.

Theory

COVID-19 represents a unique opportunity for entrepreneurship researchers to derive new information about the impact of a crisis on society. A number of theoretical perspectives in the entrepreneurship literature already show promise of being incorporated into COVID-19 research. This includes resilience theory, conflict management, and social movement. Entrepreneurship has generally been widely researched and there are a number of existing theories that are used in research studies. Nevertheless, there are still a number of new theories emerging in the literature on entrepreneurship and small business. The concept of COVID-19-related entrepreneurship has emerged from the tenets of small business strategy. While small business management is a well-researched topic, COVID-19 is new, so there is scope for further development.

COVID-19 entrepreneurship is part of the larger ecosystem of entrepreneurship research. Entrepreneurial ecosystems imply a degree of flexibility and change due to environmental conditions. This means that the exploration of COVID-19 in entrepreneurial ecosystem research will be an important contribution toward entrepreneurship theory. This will not only help to increase the share of theoretical contribution toward health crises and entrepreneurship but also cement the position of small business strategy in entrepreneurship theory. In addition, future researchers need to extend current entrepreneurship theory to a COVID-19 context. The same methods and measures can be used but adapted to suit the COVID-19 environment (Sharma, Leung, Kingshott, Davcik and Cardinali, 2020). Moreover, there are research opportunities to carry out new research regarding the impact of COVID-19 on entrepreneurship. Studies conducted at different times during the COVID-19 crisis should be conducted to analyze the differences.

Similar studies can be undertaken in various industries including airlines, education, financial services, and tourism to understand the impact of COVID-19 on entrepreneurship. The same research can be conducted in developing and emerging economies in order to assess the difference with developed countries. Moreover, there is scope for further empirical research to examine the motives for entrepreneurship during the COVID-19 crisis. Existing entrepreneurship research has explored in-depth the motivations and reasons for entrepreneurship. However, there is reason to believe these motives may change during a crisis. This is due to there being multiple explanations and reasons for being entrepreneurial during a crisis. These explanations can be referred to as antecedents for entrepreneurial behavior.

There are few existing studies that explain in-depth how entrepreneurship occurs during a crisis. This means the topic is in its formative stages and new research would be an important contribution toward theory development. COVID-19 entrepreneurship should be looked at from different theoretical perspectives including taking economics, psychology, and social science approach. When the theory about COVID-19 entrepreneurship is properly developed, it would help to explain the relationship between crises and entrepreneurship. This would enable more researchers to be motivated to engage in this area and encourage more theoretical development.

Small business leadership

Effective leadership is needed in times of crisis particularly that which takes an entrepreneurial form. Entrepreneurial leadership occurs when there is an effort by managers to proactively focus on opportunities. This means pursuing new possibilities instead of continuing with the status quo. To be entrepreneurial as a leader can take time as there needs to be a focus on how to create or discover attractive opportunities. This means proactively searching for new market possibilities before another entity follows the same path. The essence of entrepreneurial leadership involves leveraging innovation in order to design new processes. This can occur in a variety of ways but it normally involves some degree of risk-taking. Entrepreneurial leadership involves individuals guiding others in a proactive way. This means recognizing the potential of others and following through with action. The collective action of individuals can then be used to harness and innovative spirit in the marketplace. This means creating partnerships as a way to pursue opportunities. The willingness to accept risk and uncertainty is an inherent characteristic of being an entrepreneur. Entrepreneurs attempt to minimize risk by evaluating market opportunities.

The COVID-19 pandemic has required small businesses to operate in a time of great uncertainty. These changed conditions have fundamentally impacted small businesses and made them more vulnerable. Thus, more research is required on how the COVID-19 pandemic has caused both destruction and creativity to a small business strategy. The destruction comes from current business models being transformed into more digital relevant models. This has made small businesses completely rethink what they are currently doing in order to survive in the current conditions. The unpredictable nature of the COVID-19 pandemic in terms of length and impact is still unknown, which causes further hardship to small businesses. This extreme uncertainty makes it difficult for small businesses to predict future growth patterns.

There are many issues that remain unanswered and are worth exploring in terms of the impact of COVID-19 on entrepreneurship. COVID-19 was a surprise and most small businesses did not predict that it would affect the global economy. Some of the issues requiring further research involve highlighting how to understand both the positive and negative aspects of the crisis. This means small businesses can learn how to minimize the negative impacts by focusing on the positive changes.

Crisis management

In the general entrepreneurship literature, research on performance is relatively well developed. This robust stream of research acknowledges that there is importance placed on the outcomes of entrepreneurial activity. The effect of crises on entrepreneurial performance is less known particularly crises that have a health-related form. This means existing entrepreneurship theories need to incorporate more information about how crises can potentially change original thought practices. There are a few exceptions to entrepreneurship theory embedding a crisis perspective and this comes from the research on resilience. In fact, the impact of resilient behavior on entrepreneurship is becoming more known in the general body of literature about entrepreneurship. More studies are including the word 'resilience' in entrepreneurship studies that are generating new results. However, little is known about the health-related outcomes of a crisis and this oversight is considered significant. This is due to entrepreneurial organizations being better able to handle crises than other types of organizations. There is currently not much research on how entrepreneurial organizations deal with crises or the outcomes of health-related events. This will change due to the significant impact COVID-19 as a health crisis has had on entrepreneurship. As entrepreneurial organizations represent an innovative and risk-taking category of business, more information is needed about how they respond to such crises. The oversight in the entrepreneurship literature on health crises is particularly relevant and should be addressed in more detail. This will provide a further sense of clarity about the role of crises in entrepreneurship studies.

Entrepreneurship and the global marketplace

There is a need for small businesses to be entrepreneurial in order to ensure their longevity in the market. Entrepreneurship is an engine for growth and is needed in the global marketplace. In a small business, entrepreneurship denotes significant change in the way work is conducted. In the COVID-19 context, there is a growing body of work investigating the determinants of entrepreneurship. This involves assessing the knowledge sources needed in introducing an entrepreneurial mindset into the marketplace. Small businesses depend on different types of knowledge sources for new ideas. Knowledge sources enable the transfer of commercially sensitive information without the need for formal contracts. This enables specific information about new production processes or market development to be obtained.

Dawson, Fountain and Cohen (2011:352) state 'a broadened view of entrepreneurship recognizes entrepreneurship as a process, highlighting the importance of context in the mix and incorporating cultural, economic, geographical, political and social factors.' This means the environment influences how entrepreneurship is conducted in society. Entrepreneurship is not just an economic activity but is also the result of individual motivations. While the use of the term 'entrepreneurship' varies, at its essence is the idea that business activity can contribute to social and economic goals. Historically entrepreneurship has been associated with economics and industrialization but this has altered with renewed interest in social responsibility. As a result, the entrepreneurship literature now includes theories from marketing, psychology, and sociology.

Therefore, these theories need to be utilized in new research that incorporates a COVID-19 perspective.

Small business resilience

Resilience is defined as 'the capacity of a system to absorb disturbance and reorganize while undergoing change so as to still remain essentially the same function, structure, identity and feedbacks' (Walker, Holling, Carpenter and Kinzig, 2004:4). In order to maintain resilience there needs to be some form of adaptation and transformation. This is due to the need to think in new ways about changing dynamics occurring in the environment. The term 'resilience' refers to the capacity to go back to a normal state after some kind of disturbance. Resilience is an important behavior characteristic that enables an individual to transform and adjust to new conditions. This means adapting to environmental change by retaining the same function. General resilience refers to the ability to adjust to all kinds of shock so this needs to be researched in more detail taking into account the COVID-19 crisis.

Resilience involves having the capacity to adjust to disturbances that threaten the current conditions. Resilience is based on an accumulation of personal characteristics that enable survivability in times of hardship. This means having a competence when under stressful conditions. Some individuals become resilient based on their experience in dealing with change. This means resilience may refer to positive functioning after a traumatic event. Therefore, resilience can be a developmental outcome and refers to coping mechanisms. Resilience occurs in the presence of adversity as an individual adapts to change. Masten and Powell (2003:4) refer to resilience as 'patterns of positive adaptation in the context of significant risk or adversity.' Resilience is influenced by the interactions an individual has in their natural environment. This means the environment plays a key role in an individual being able to be resilient. Resilience is related to the protective and vulnerability faced by an individual in the environment. Therefore, resilience cannot be understood by just focusing on an individual as it is related to community and social factors. This means that there are environmental conditions that lead to individuals being able to better function in adverse situations. Thus, some individuals are better able to adapt by being more competent and stronger.

Crises are complex and can differ in terms of impact so future research needs to examine this path. Natural disasters such as earthquakes and hurricanes tend to occur on a frequent and reoccurring basis. Other types of crises such as terrorism and war are less frequent but still have an enormous impact on society. Entrepreneurship in times of crisis is not the same as other time periods due to the need for urgent action. This means crises represent a new kind of environment that business needs to respond to and related research needs to focus on this topic. Crises research regarding entrepreneurship is a new area of study. As a field of study crisis management has already been given a prominent setting in other business management fields. This is due to a crisis being classified by its unexpected nature and low probability of occurring. This means a crisis can be considered as an unpredictable event that occurs over a specific time period. Therefore, a crisis disrupts the normal functioning of an environment by altering everyday activities. This means over time a crisis affects society in different ways. Thus, new research about how entrepreneurs are needed in times of crisis in order to adapt to new conditions is required. During a crisis, entrepreneurs try to mitigate its effects by developing new business ventures. Entrepreneurs respond to changes by taking action instead of carrying on with business as normal.

Social resilience refers to how the community responds to change. This topic needs to be studied in more detail particularly in terms of disadvantaged members of society in times of the COVID-19 crisis. Social vulnerability can be described as 'the exposure of groups of people or individuals to stress a result of the impacts of environmental change' (Adger, 2000:348). This means that individuals who are forced to adapt to the changing physical environment are considered vulnerable. These changes affect individual's livelihoods and disrupt other social activities. Thus, research should study how vulnerability can occur when individuals are stressed and foresee irreversible change. This is caused by human or environmental change that causes risks. A resilient individual will be able to better cope with stress. Resilience is hard to observe as it is a psychological trait. It can be considered as a buffer capacity in that an individual can absorb disruptions.

Suggestions for policy makers

Policy makers have focused on trying to help existing businesses due to their effect on the employment rate. It is necessary for policymakers to address and understand challenges faced by entrepreneurs. This is due to the way entrepreneurs can learn from each other in terms of ways to survive. To manage the COVID-19 crisis, entrepreneurs need to have a strategic plan in terms of what they are doing and how or if this will change in the future. This means choosing which actions to take in light of the COVID-19 situation and whether this should change in light of changing conditions.

Policy makers are grappling with how to do deal with the economic and social repercussions of the COVID-19 virus. The public health strategy of social distancing helps to decrease transmission rates but comes at a cost. These costs include the associated social and psychological trauma in dealing with the change. Health-related crises impact business in various ways. Directly a health crisis impacts the operation of a business and indirectly through personal well-being. Governments around the world have focused on saving the lives of citizens. However, the impact of COVID-19 on the global economy is estimated to be more than previous recessions. This means consideration is required on the challenges entrepreneurs face during the COVID-19 crisis as they have not yet been scrutinized due to the time lag between practice and scholarship.

Just a few studies have been published on COVID-19 and entrepreneurship, although this is expected to change in the future. More entrepreneurs are ramping up their efforts to be adaptable based on current market conditions. A policy question remains unanswered: in the scholarship and practice of entrepreneurship what are the challenges faced by entrepreneurs in the crisis? Most of the support measures used by governments have focused on established businesses rather than startups. This means the emphasis is on trying to save existing businesses through rent subsidies or tax exemptions rather than promoting the use of startups. Entrepreneurs are among the most vulnerable in the COVID-19 environment due to their need to access finance and resources. The situation for entrepreneurs particularly in emerging economies is complicated due to the difference in public health facilities compared to developed countries. This has meant emerging economies including India and Brazil have had high levels of COVID-19 infections that have hampered the ability of entrepreneurs. In particular, informal entrepreneurs in emerging economies have been especially affected due to many relying on the tourism sector. This has caused social problems in emerging economies that do not have the same level of social services existing in developed countries. Not all emerging economies have been affected in the same way with countries like Thailand and Vietnam having low rates of infection. Therefore, future research policy needs to examine separately issues related to management, support, factors, and performance. Suggestions for each theme are stated in Table 9.2.

Table 9.2 Suggestions for policy makers regarding future research

Theme	*Suggestions*
Crisis management process	Develop and test new approaches for understanding how entrepreneurs manage the crisis.
	Study the crisis management approach launched at various stages during the crisis.
Support process	To determine the support needed to help entrepreneurs establish new businesses.
	To understand how entrepreneurs can continue and sustain their businesses.
	To analyze case studies of success in order for other entrepreneurs to learn by example.
Specific factors influencing entrepreneurship	To investigate the role of different types of entrepreneurship that involves products and services related to COVID-19.
	To understand the preferred modes of entrepreneurship.
	To compare family versus nonfamily-owned businesses.
	To research the role of digital technology in entrepreneurship.
Entrepreneurship and performance	To understand the link between entrepreneurial activity and financial performance.
	To compare and contrast different performance rates based on industry sectors.
	To analyze whether the stage of the COVID-19 crisis in terms of severity influenced the performance rate of the entrepreneurs.

Source: Author developed.

Managerial implications

In order to understand what is meant by COVID-19 entrepreneurship, first the definition of COVID-19 and entrepreneurship needs to be explained in terms of managerial relevance. COVID-19 is slowing down the global economy by affecting everyday life and small business managers have had to grapple with new circumstances. There are many economic effects from the COVID-19 pandemic including the disruption to the supply chain of products and services. This has meant a reduction in firm's cash flow and ability to pay for supplies. In addition, there have been losses in international business trade due to decreased flight schedules. Social consequences of COVID-19 include the cancellation of sport and music events, closure of restaurants, and disruption of community activities. This has affected the way individuals live and influences their social activities. Fornaro and Wolf (2020) suggest that drastic policy interventions might be needed to prevent economic catastrophes. This includes making changes to fiscal and monetary policy in order to spur economic activity. Thus, small business managers need to consider policy change as well as implement practical change in order to survive.

The COVID-19 pandemic created high levels of risk for financial market investors. The lockdown strategy imposed by many cities due to the COVID-19 pandemic has affected the stock prices of major companies. The COVID-19 crisis is affecting all segments of the global population including poor, middle class, and rich. Vulnerable people especially the elderly have been most affected as they are highly susceptible to the disease. The COVID-19 pandemic brings a new context into how small business managers can prosper during the crisis. The rules for entrepreneurship change based on the time and place of the business activity. Social entrepreneurship can be practiced by small business managers during the crisis as it refers to more human relationships that are based on kindness. This means the emphasis on social entrepreneurship is more at the micro level by incorporating some form of nonprofit activity into business ventures. Societal entrepreneurship refers to a more macro context as it examines how society functions based on entrepreneurial occurrences. This means the context of societal entrepreneurship considers the interaction occurring among a variety of entities in the environment.

Conclusion

The main purpose of this chapter is to critically analyze the topic of entrepreneurship, small business, and COVID-19. COVID-19 and small business entrepreneurship research is relatively new and a novel topic. There is potential for more research to focus on the relationship between these topics and how they affect societal development. Moreover, there should be more research cross-culturally comparing different perspectives regarding COVID-19. This will enable new research to emerge from a different angle. This chapter has discussed how there is a need for more in-depth directions for future research.

Each of the chapters in this book makes a unique empirical and theoretical contribution to the emerging literature on COVID-19 entrepreneurship. Collectively the chapters suggest that COVID-19 entrepreneurship will push the entrepreneurship field into new directions. This means focusing on the purpose of entrepreneurship including the reason for action and the context. Thereby helping to understand how individual demand for products and services in a COVID-19 context influences interest in entrepreneurship. The chapters highlight the importance of a COVID-19 dominant logic for emerging entrepreneurship research. This is critical in ensuring research focuses on how to provide support structures and funding to entrepreneurs in times of a crisis. This research is expected to have a substantial impact on the development of COVID-19 entrepreneurship in the global economy.

References

Adger, W. N. (2000) 'Social and ecological resilience: Are they related?', *Progress in Human Geography*, 24(3): 347–364.

Akkermans, J., Richardson, J. and Kraimer, M. (2020) 'The Covid-19 crisis as a career shock: Implications for careers and vocational behaviour', *Journal of Vocational Behavior*, In Press.

Alon, I., Farrell, M. and Li, S. (2020) 'Regime type and Covid-19 response', *FIIB Business Review*, 1–9. https://doi.org/10.1177/2319714520928884

Ansell, C. and Boin, A. (2019) 'Taming deep uncertainty: The potential of pragmatist principles for understanding and improving strategic crisis management', *Administration & Society*, 51(7): 1079–1112.

Bailey, K. and Breslin, D. (2020) 'The Covid-19 pandemic: What can we learn from past research in organisations and management?', *International Journal of Management Reviews*, In Press.

Brammer, S. and Clark, T. (2020) 'Covid-19 and management education: Reflections on challenges, opportunities, and potential futures', *British Journal of Management*, 31: 453–456.

Brinks, V. and Ibert, O. (2020) 'From coronavirus to coronacrisis: The value of an analytical and geographical understanding of crisis', *Tijdschrift voor Economische en Sociale Geografie*, 1–13.

Brown, R. and Rocha, A. (2020) 'Entrepreneurial uncertainty during the Covid-19 crisis: Mapping the temporal dynamics of entrepreneurial finance', *Journal of Business Venturing Insights*, In Press.

Buchanan, D. A. and Denyer, D. (2013) 'Researching tomorrow's crisis: Methodological innovations and wider implications', *International Journal of Management Reviews*, 15(2): 205–224.

Cortez, R. and Johnston, W. (2020) 'The coronavirus crisis in B2B settings: Crisis uniqueness and managerial implications based on social exchange theory', *Industrial Marketing Management*, In Press.

Dawson, D., Fountain, J. and Cohen, D. A. (2011) 'Seasonality and the lifestyle "conundrum": An analysis of lifestyle entrepreneurship in wine tourism regions', *Asia Pacific Journal of Tourism Research*, 16(5): 551–572.

Doern, R. (2016) 'Entrepreneurship and crisis management: The experiences of small businesses during the London 2011 riots', *International Small Business Journal*, 34(3): 276–302.

Donthu, N. and Gustafsson, A. (2020) 'Effects of Covid-19 on business and research', *Journal of Business Research*, 117: 284–289.

Eggers, F. (2020) 'Masters of disasters? Challenges and opportunities for SMEs in times of crisis', *Journal of Business Research*, 116(1): 199–208.

Faulkner, B. (2001) 'Towards a framework for tourism disaster management', *Tourism Management*, 22(2): 135–147.

Ferreira, J. J., Fayolle, A., Ratten, V. and Raposo, M. (Eds.). (2018) *Entrepreneurial universities*. Cheltenham, United Kingdom: Edward Elgar Publishing.

Ferreira, J. J., Fernandes, C. I. and Ratten, V. (2017) 'The influence of entrepreneurship education on entrepreneurial intentions', In *Entrepreneurial universities* (pp. 19–34). Cham: Springer.

Fornaro, L. and Wolf, M. (2020) *Covid-19 coronavirus and macroeconomic policy*, www.crei.cat/wp-content/uploads/2020/03/C19-1.pdf, last visited 18th October 2020.

Hall, C. M., Scott, D. and Gössling, S. (2020) 'Pandemics, transformations and tourism: Be careful what you wish for', *Tourism Geographies*, In Press.

He, H. and Harris, L. (2020) 'The impact of Covid-19 pandemic on corporate social responsibility and marketing philosophy', *Journal of Business Research*, In Press.

Higgins-Desbiolles, F. (2020) 'Socialising tourism for social and ecological justice after Covid-19', *Tourism Geographies*, In Press.

Hills, A. (1998) 'Seduced by recovery: The consequences of misunderstanding disaster', *Journal of Contingencies and Crisis Management*, 6(3): 162–170.

Jeyanathan, M., Afkhami, S., Smaill, F., Miller, M. S., Lichty, B. D. and Xing, Z. (2020) 'Immunological considerations for Covid-19 vaccine strategies', *Nature Reviews Immunology*, 1–18.

Jones, P., Jones, A., Williams-Burnett, N. and Ratten, V. (2017) 'Let's get physical: Stories of entrepreneurial activity from sports coaches/instructors', *The International Journal of Entrepreneurship and Innovation*, 18(4): 219–230.

Jones, P., Klapper, R., Ratten, V. and Fayolle, A. (2018) 'Emerging themes in entrepreneurial behaviours, identities and contexts', *The International Journal of Entrepreneurship and Innovation*, 19(4): 233–236.

Jones, P., Ratten, V., Klapper, R. and Fayolle, A. (2019) 'Entrepreneurial identity and context: Current trends and an agenda for future research', *The International Journal of Entrepreneurship and Innovation*, 20(1): 3–7.

Kirk, C. P. and Rifkin, S. (2020) 'I'll trade you diamonds for toilet paper: Consumer reacting, coping and adapting behaviors in the Covid-19 pandemic', *Journal of Business Research*, In Press.

Kraus, S., Clauss, T., Breier, M., Gast, J., Zardini, A. and Tiberius, V. (2020) 'The economics of Covid-19: Initial empirical evidence on how family firms in five European countries cope with the corona crisis', *International Journal of Entrepreneurial Behavior & Research*, In Press.

Krishnamurthy, S. (2020) 'The future of business education: A commentary in the shadow of the Covid-19 pandemic', *Journal of Business Research*, 117: 1–5.

Kuckertz, A., Brändle, L., Gaudig, A., Hinderer, S., Reyes, C. A. M., Prochotta, A. and Berger, E. S. (2020) 'Startups in times of crisis – A rapid response to the Covid-19 pandemic', *Journal of Business Venturing Insights*, In Press.

Liguori, E. and Winkler, C. (2020) 'From offline to online: Challenges and opportunities for entrepreneurship education following the Covid-19 pandemic', *Entrepreneurship Education and Pedagogy*, In Press.

Liu, Y., Shankar, V. and Yun, W. (2017) 'Crisis management strategies and the long-term effects of product recalls on firm value', *Journal of Marketing*, 81(September): 30–48.

Marshall, A. and Wolanskyj-Spinner, A. (2020) 'Covid-19: Challenges and opportunities for educators and generation Z learners', *Mayo Clinical Proceedings*, 95(6): 1135–1137.

Masten, A. S. and Powell, J. L. (2003) 'A resilience framework for research, policy, and practice', In S. S. Luthar (Ed.), *Resilience and vulnerability: Adaptation in the context of childhood adversities* (pp. 1–28). New York: Cambridge University Press.

Parnell, D., Widdop, P., Bond, A. and Wilson, R. (2020) 'Covid-19, networks and sport', *Managing Sport and Leisure*, In Press.

Ratten, V. (2017) 'Entrepreneurial universities: The role of communities, people and places', *Journal of Enterprising Communities: People and Places in the Global Economy*, 11(3): 310–315.

Ratten, V. and Jones, P. (2018) 'Future research directions for sport education: Toward an entrepreneurial learning approach', *Education+ Training*, 60(5): 490–499.

Sharma, P., Leung, T. Y., Kingshott, R. P., Davcik, N. S. and Cardinali, S. (2020) 'Managing uncertainty during a global pandemic: An international business perspective', *Journal of Business Research*, 116(1): 188–192.

Walker, B., Holling, C. S., Carpenter, S. R. and Kinzig, A. (2004) 'Resilience, adaptability and transformability in social – Ecological systems', *Ecology and Society*, 9(2): 5.

Wen, J., Wang, W., Kozak, M., Liu, X. and Hou, H. (2020) 'Many brains are better than one: The importance of interdisciplinary studies on Covid-19 in and beyond tourism', *Tourism Recreation Research*, In Press.

Index

Printed in the United States
by Baker & Taylor Publisher Services